OREGON
Rediscovered

by Joe Bianco

with editorial assistance of
Art Chenoweth

Benedictine Press

and

JRB Publishing Company

Library of Congress Cataloging-in-Publication Data

Bianco, Joe.
    Oregon rediscovered / by Joe Bianco ;
with editorial assistance by Art Chenoweth. —
Portland, Or. : Benedictine Press : Joseph R.
Bianco Pub., c1994.
      p. : ill., map ; cm.
   ISBN: 0-9643408-0-1
    1. Oregon—Description and travel—
Guidebooks.   2. Oregon—History—Miscellanea.
I. Title.
F874.3.B   917.95'04 dc20

10 9 8 7 6 5 4 3 2 1

Table
of
Contents

Foreword

No single book can possibly describe the Oregon character in all of its many facets, both historical and contemporary. But Joe Bianco has captured the essence of the Oregon experience as well as anyone who has tried.

Indeed, Bianco does offer a fresh look at a much-traveled landscape and most especially its varied mix of peoples and their cultures. What comes through the well-organized chapters is the excitement of discovery that he experienced after moving to Oregon as a wide-eyed and curious young reporter.

Bianco's enthusiasm for what he has encountered is infectious, clearly coloring the variety of legends and stories that are set forth humorously and accurately. His commentaries on how Oregon has changed over the past 35 years and how living in Oregon has changed him are illuminating.

For the first time adventurer or traveler through the Oregon cityscape and countryside, Bianco offers personalized recommendations of where to go and how to get there and what you find when you get there.

Previously best known as a devotee of the culinary arts, here he serves up a different meal—food for thought. In fact, the entire book is a delightful repast that should be enjoyed by all Oregonians, both old-timers and newcomers, who want to gain deeper insights into the true Oregon character.

E. Kimbark MacColl
Portland, Oregon

Acknowledgments

Oregon has changed and matured so much since I first arrived here more than 35 years ago that I decided it was time to revisit and rediscover the wonders of this immensely beautiful state and write about them.

I suggested this to my publisher, Oral Bullard of Touchstone Press, and he accepted and supported me. Sadly, he did not live to see the book finished. His company went out of business shortly thereafter. However, I dedicate this work to his memory, for he was the one who encouraged me early in my book-writing career.

It has taken almost five years to complete this book, and I am deeply grateful to my friends, who maintained their contacts with me whenever I retreated for periods to my lonely carrel at Mt. Angel Library.

A special thanks to my friend, John D. Ryan, who drove me to many parts of Oregon while extolling the beauty of this state. Whenever we traveled about, either gathering bits of data or taking pictures, I was always amazed at the depth of his affection for his native Oregon. It only inspired me further to complete this book.

I dedicate this book also to my children, Martha and Joey, both Oregon natives, and to their mother, my late wife, Yvonne Gault Bianco, who rests in the soils of this great state. And I dedicate it to those who already live here and to those who will follow their dreams and make living in Oregon a happy realization.

Further thanks are due those who cooperated in the research: to the monks at Mt. Angel Abbey, who so graciously granted the use of their library; to several Indian tribes of this state—the Confederated Tribes of Warm Springs, the Confederated Tribes of Siletz, the Confederated Tribes of Grande Ronde, and the Confederated Tribes of Umatilla—and to Bill Ray of the Klamath Tribe, who opened the first door; to the folks at the Oregon State

Tourism Office; to Anthony Yturri, my Basque friend from Ontario, Oregon, who, with his wife, showed me the way of the Basques; and to all the others who made it possible.

A special thanks to my former colleagues at *The Oregonian*, to my book executive editor, Art Chenoweth, and to Peggy, for being there.

Onward to Oregon.

Oregon
Rediscovered

Introduction

*A big city boy from the
East grows webbed feet—
and loves it*

I was going to begin this book with a description of Oregon, land of the Douglas fir, the cedar, and the hemlock, of swift clear-running rivers and a cold green-blue ocean. But if I had done so, readers might have had considerable difficulty in distinguishing this book from the many other well-deserved tributes to this state, some of them written by far more experienced historians and storytellers than I.

Consequently, this book is not only about Oregon but also about me and how this land finally captivated me, a young man from the sidewalks of Newark. My love affair with this state began reluctantly many years ago, and there were both good times and bad times, but gradually a bond developed that now cannot be broken.

I never intended originally to write about myself. It was my thought simply to show others how Oregon is changing and how to reach and enjoy all those attractions, whether near or distant, that have made this state unforgettable to those who come here. But I believe that for the reader to delight in what brings joy to me, I must begin with who I am and why I want to share my personal journey with others. Therefore this book, while not an autobiography, will be a frank look at both myself and my adopted state.

I remember that when I first came here in the 1950s, I rejected and yes, even despised some things. That I now can attribute to a self-indulgent youth and a natural laziness which found itself facing too many sacrifices. Through the years I have learned that some people can live without friends, without luxuries, even without the arts and recreations of city life, as long as they can walk through the woods and enjoy the singing of just one bird.

My story begins with a small, big-brown-eyed and curly-black-haired youth who had a dream so big it had to come true, even though he was to be ostracized by his parents and siblings for breaking with a tradition. You see, I grew up in what is today referred to by sociologists as an ethnic family. The Italo-Americans were the Hispanics or the Asians of 50 years ago, along with the Irish and others who came to this country.

Our family was one body, and my father and mother were its heart. Whatever we did was governed by them. We all looked to our parents for approval, and even to this day I still find myself wanting that gesture of approval from my father, who is in his 90s. My mother died several years ago, but until the day she died the authority in that family was shared equally by her and my father. With such a strong family, and with very strong convictions of my own, I knew who would be carrying the cross if I made a break from centuries of strict European behavior.

Growing up an Italo-American in a mixed neighborhood meant work at an early age, school, and little time or means left over for more casual pursuits. Yet somehow, no matter how I devoted myself to work and school, I found myself desiring the company of the opposite sex, as far back as I can remember. The reason I am telling all this is because it has a bearing on how and why I came to Oregon and made it my home.

When I was very young, my mother warned me that I would one day "marry for a cake." At this early age I found out you cannot fool your mother. Mothers are all-knowing; and mine was no different. She was uncanny when it came to listening to my thoughts. My predilection for sweets was no secret to her.

I remember vividly one evening many years ago when we were sitting at the supper table, having our usual midweek meal which my mother had so ingeniously prepared. We were all there: my father, my sister, my younger brother and, of course, my mother, who was always the center of attention.

My father did not talk much at the supper table. He would listen as my mother recounted the events of the day and reviewed, with her innate knack for drama, the daily conduct of each of her children.

During one of these supper discourses there came an unexpected knock at the kitchen door. It had to be someone we knew; otherwise the caller would have used the front entrance. It was a neighbor with a harried look on his face. In his uneasiness he forgot to apologize for his intrusion.

"I've come for my daughter's photograph. She wants it back."

All eyes turned to me. Then, my father turned to me. He did not open his mouth, but from the way he looked at me, I knew what he was thinking.

I hurried to my room and returned, slightly shaken, to hand the small passport-sized photograph to Laura's father. He took it and said, "Good night."

The remainder of the meal was passed in silence except for my father's sudden command: "Tonight you will stay in. Maybe tomorrow, too." My father had spoken.

"As I said many times, Pepe (little Guiseppe), one of these days you will marry for a cake." It was my mother, adding a little comic relief.

* * *

It was during those early years that I began thinking about living in the West. I resented being restricted by anyone. I had heard about the freedom in the West. I still can remember sitting on the porch of Petite's candy store in Newark, looking at the afternoon sun setting softly in the west and wondering about the excitement of living out there.

My dream began to come true sooner than I had expected. While I was a student at Seton Hall University in New Jersey, one of my fellow students, who was chief copy boy at the city's morning newspaper, the *Star-Ledger*, offered me a copyboy job. I took it. It was this decision that eventually brought me to Oregon.

* * *

Meanwhile, the job market was shrinking. I asked my boss, the city editor, whether there would be any reporter jobs available when I graduated. I had now been working there for three years and had six months to go for graduation. He said there would be, but not in Newark. I would need to go to one of our sister newspapers in Harrisburg, Pennsylvania.

The only catch, he told me, was that I had to take the job right away. That meant leaving school in my senior year, which I did. I never graduated and never went back to live in Newark. I had flown the coop.

It was not a happy day for my parents, for it was difficult for them to see their oldest son leave. And to make matters more difficult, I eventually met someone who offered me that proverbial cake. It was not the marriage that displeased my parents but the fact that my young wife came from Oregon, which then was as far and as foreign to an easterner as China. Any time we talked about moving away from New Jersey and heading west, my father would always say, "If you want to move that far, why not move to China?"

Oregon was not China, but to many easterners it was barely the United

States. My parents knew that sooner or later I would be heading down that old Oregon trail because they knew that most women wanted to be close to their parents, particularly during the early years of marriage. And in fact it didn't take long before I was heading west.

While I was in Harrisburg, the owners of the newspaper announced the purchase of a newspaper in Oregon. It was the only newspaper they ever bought in the West, but it was the beginning of the S.I. Newhouse chain of newspapers.

Within a few years, as my parents had forewarned, I was on my way to Oregon and the start of a new life and career in an entirely different culture. The time was the 1950s, and television had not yet homogenized the nation. Living in Oregon then was living in a different culture. The only resemblance to my home back in New Jersey was that English was spoken.

When I came to Oregon, I couldn't find anything that could remind me of home. My favorite Italian foods were not to be found. It was mostly a meat and potato society. Italian vegetables were rare and you had to hunt for them.

Shortly after I came to Oregon, a New Yorker from Brooklyn tried to introduce pizza to Portlanders. He called himself "Sam, the pizza man." There were no takers.

Bagels? Even though bagels weren't Italian, they reminded me of my youth growing up in a mixed neighborhood. But the stores in the Portland area didn't stock them. You could find them only in what was then "Old South Portland," in the Jewish neighborhood on SW First and Second Avenues near Sheridan Street.

Portland in those years was terribly lacking in ethnic foods. Searching even for a can of Italian tomatoes was a treasure hunt. Such items existed only in the few Italian delis operated by Italians such as the Colistros and Colasuonnos, early-day Italian merchant families.

Everyone who lived in Oregon then seemed to be a native. There were few out-of-state people. Most of the reporters and editors on our staff came from the Northwest and primarily from Oregon. Also, although today there is a mixture of many nationalities and races in Oregon, in the 1950s there were mostly just Scandinavians, Germans, and some Irish. I was an outsider, and at times I felt like a second-class citizen. I was tolerated but kept at a distance.

What was amusing to me were the misconceptions people had of easterners, particularly if you happened to be of a strong ethnic background. They used to lump us all together. I remember a woman reporter in Salem who couldn't tell a person's nationality by the surname and thought that if I came from the New York area I had to be Jewish. I told her that although there were Italian Jews, like Dr. Enrico Fermi (one of the developers of the first atom bomb), I was not one of them. I don't remember if I detected a sigh of relief or a lessening of suspicion, but I soon was able to assure her that easterners were not what she had made us out to be.

When we first arrived, Oregon was barely 100 years old as a state. Choice real estate in prime residential areas of Portland was still available from the county government. Raw land in the city was available for about $10 a month at low interest, about 5 percent, from the county land office in Portland.

I put a $10 down-payment on almost a half-block in what is now an upscale residential property area in Willamette Heights. The price tag then for what is now four 10,000-square-foot lots was $2,500, and there were few takers. There was a virtually untapped reservoir of land in the city that had not caught the eye of the developer.

There were berry fields then all over Gresham. The city was known as the "Berry Capital" of the state. There were no tract houses, just open fields.

Oregonians had an aversion to growth, and they felt that much of the land around the city, even in the West Hills, should remain in its natural pristine state. What happened to that pristine undeveloped land is now history.

The tallest building in Portland at that time was the Public Service Building, home of the Pacific Power & Light Company. There was nothing else.

The skyline was the West Hills. You could see Mt. Hood from the Portland Towers and from the Ione Plaza and Park Plaza, all apartment buildings in the downtown area. Those were the "big highrises" back then.

Restaurants of four-star quality and hotels of equal luster were rare, if not nonexistent. In Portland, the spot to go after the movie was Jolly Joan on SW Broadway or Yaw's Top Notch hamburger place in the Hollywood district.

There wasn't a lot of big-city glamour, but one memory of that kind stands out for me: the opening night of "Forever Amber" at J. J. Parker's Broadway Theater, where the Broadway Building now stands. The event was a benefit for Boys Town of Italy, and Linda Darnell, who starred in it, came from Hollywood to Portland for the celebration. I was the one who picked her up at the airport and escorted her to the opening, and I remember that she was ravishing. It was like Academy Awards night in Hollywood, except that the crowds were smaller and there were only a few stars. Nevertheless, it was a dazzling spectacle for Portland in those days.

In those quiet years of the 1950s, Portland and the rest of the state possessed a distinct personality, devoid of pretense. The state had charm, and slowly and surely it turned even the most ardent foes into Oregonians proud of their web feet. I resisted at first when my wife tried to convert me to being an Oregonian: I still had my ties to the East, and I felt that even though it was overcrowded, it was still the place to enjoy life. But my only link there was with my family, my parents. Now, as I started to raise my own family, my allegiance gradually shifted more to Oregon. As I began to discover for myself its many treasures, I began freeing myself from the past. It was hard for me, but I was compelled to make that break. And when I did, it was therapeutically exalting.

I remember that at first I had trouble getting used to the rain. The natives called it "mist" or "liquid sunshine," but calling rain "mist" did nothing to soothe my homesick soul.

Go to the beach, I was told. Drive to the mountains. Fish! Hike! Camp! Visit state parks! These suggestions from the long-time Oregon residents sounded more like impossible directives. How can one hike, camp outdoors, fish, and do all those activities outdoors when it always rains, I asked. Well, you do them regardless.

I learned it was the only way, and soon I began growing the proverbial webbing between my toes. Today, I am attracted to the north side of anything. And moss? It's my favorite plant. I am a confirmed Oregonian, baptized by the rain.

Nothing makes me happier than to wake up and see clouds overhead and the temperature leveling off around the 60s. When summer comes and the weather changes from mild to very hot, I escape to the shade and secretly pray for cooler weather. My home is on the leeward side of the hill, and my favorite view is north, enhanced by Mt. St. Helens, which is in full view from every one of my windows.

When I pushed aside my first instinct to dislike Oregon because of the rain and the distance from my family, I started to see why most people who came before me from other parts of the country never returned to their origins.

I started to notice how I spoke of Oregon when I visited my parents back east. I would talk about the expansive beauty and the feeling of freedom. It was a spiritual freedom, a natural freedom. You never felt hemmed in. As the years passed, I talked more and more about why I liked Oregon. I never thought I would do it, but I did. It was the trips on the weekends that I took with my wife and two kids that cemented my relationship to the state. We would pack a lunch, put the kids in the back of our station wagon, and go exploring.

So now begins what I can recall of our early days in Oregon, when we turned our weekends into adventures.

We began by exploring the Columbia River from Portland east through that massive and geologically impressive gorge, a spectacle which could bring sighs of admiration from even the most worldly of travelers. It was unique, and the Columbia River made it so. I used to hear about the Columbia when I was a youngster, but I could not believe the beauty of this river the first time I saw it.

The Mississippi, which was the famous river from early high school geography days, looked tired and gray in comparison to the Columbia. This river looked young and strong, and its color was a deep blue with ripples of white caps to give it a distinguished look.

The Columbia was a river which had youthful force, fed by the mighty Gorge east winds. These winds would, in later years, attract wind surfers from around the world and turn the quiet farming community of Hood River into the aqua-rollercoasting capital of the world.

For weeks in the summer we traveled the Gorge, each time venturing farther and farther east. It was all magnificent, from the many waterfalls along the Oregon side of the Columbia to Beacon Rock on the Washington side—the second largest monolith of its kind in the world.

We could hike the trails along the old Columbia River Highway, or just look for a quiet place off the beaten path to rest our picnic basket and ourselves. At Multnomah Falls, we would stand in awe as tons and tons of cascading water roared down the side of the high cliff. Sometimes we would climb the trail and walk under the falls where we could feel the cooling spray—a marvelous refreshment on a hot summer day.

We always took the old highway back to Portland through Corbett to avoid the main highway traffic below. It gave us a good view of Beacon Rock, and also took us to Crown Point, still one of the best vantage points to see the Gorge and take pictures. Crown Point is not as frequented now as it was when I first came to Oregon. Now most tourists bypass it because they prefer the faster highway at river level.

On some weekends we would be more daring, at least for this easterner, and head as far east as The Dalles and beyond, for we remembered that when we had arrived in the early 1950s we had seen Indians fishing, with long poles and nets, off platforms high above the Celilo Falls on the Columbia. We had never seen anything like this before and we wanted to go back. It was exciting to me because the only thoughts I had about the Indians were formed by John Wayne movies.

The Indians we saw were those who lived along the river. They were the Celilo Tribe, and they earned their livelihood as their ancestors had, by fishing for salmon. They were carrying on their tradition, a tradition that predates the arrival of the white man.

Seeing the Indians fish from their high platforms was somehow fascinating. I recall the tourists just sitting in their cars or standing along the viewpoint, watching the Indians for hours. I did the same. I don't know whether it was the attraction of watching the roaring river tumbling over the falls carrying its abundance of salmon or the fact that we were watching "real live Indians."

The Indians didn't mind the audience. They simply went on with their work, and when the sun got too hot, they retreated into their small nearby cabins where they could still watch their nets and maybe watch us. They would stay inside for a while and then come out and check to see if they had caught any fish.

Today the fishing grounds we saw are buried under placid river water held back by hydroelectric dams feeding power to a growing population.

An alternate journey was to Mt. Hood. A favorite day trip for us in those days was going around Mt. Hood to Hood River, particularly during the fall months. There wasn't too much traffic then, and there was always a fresh fruit farm stand along the Mt. Hood Loop road to brighten the trip.

The Hood River Valley was blessed with an abundance of orchards, mostly apples. We always made sure to pick up several bags on the way home. They were crisp, delicious apples, the kind that grew in Washington.

We also stopped at Bonneville Dam for a close view of the migrating salmon. You could watch them leap up ladders on their way to the spawning grounds.

Another favorite weekend entertainment involved driving to the coast. There you could watch the whales migrating north or stay at the coastal state parks or eat a picnic lunch in the car while we watched a storm at sea. It didn't make any difference what the weather was at the coast because you knew you couldn't swim in the ocean anyway. It was too rough and also too cold. Wetsuits and surfing were not popular at that time. But you could just relax and look at the ocean, or go clamming or crabbing, or play in the sand with your kids. Or you could buy salmon at Astoria from the fishermen and bring it down to Seaside and cook it on the beach over an open fire.

If you wanted to spend the night at the coast, there was always the state park. Camping spots were always open. You didn't have to wait for them or get reservations. The grounds were well kept, and you could put up your tent or sleep in your station wagon. The restroom facilities were clean and safe.

Most of the travelers in the state parks were Oregonians, and a few were from Washington. In the summer you occasionally would see a California license or two. Rarely would there be someone from the East Coast.

One of our favorite coastal places to stay was Florence. The kids loved the sand dunes, and we could stay at Oswald West State Park. Oswald West was the Oregon governor who protected our coast and prohibited private ownership of Oregon beaches. If it hadn't been for him, we would not have the freedom of the beaches today.

By contrast, in my home state of New Jersey you pay to go swimming in the ocean and even to spread a blanket on the sand. In Oregon we don't have to pay, and I hope we never do.

Depoe Bay was another favorite spot. There was a settlement of small cabins, and the owner, a Mr. Anderson, lived in one of them. The cabins were heated by old iron wood stoves, not like the wood stoves you see today. They had several metal plates on the top, which we cooked on. There was nothing better than cooking on a wood stove in the middle of winter, on a point overlooking the ocean.

Fishing for rock bass in the cove below our cabin was a treasured secret. I used to sit on a rock, look out at the ocean, and let my mind wander a bit. My wife, meantime, enjoyed reading by the wood stove. She knew I would always return with a good catch for dinner. The rock bass were pinkish, and when fried in the skillet they turned white. They tasted great. I've never had anything like them since.

The smell of freshly cooked fish, the burning logs in the stove, and the rain pattering on the wooden roof were the makings of a typical Oregon coast evening. We started on fish, potato chips, carrots, and beer. What a meal! What an evening!

On one of our visits to Depoe Bay we learned of a lot for sale, not too far from the cabin, near the edge of the cliff. We thought about buying that lot. It cost $2,000, which at that time was a lot of money, but I had the money saved.

In the end, though, I bought instead a small monthly newspaper in Portland because I thought it would be good to have a side job while I worked for the daily in town.

Today a lot like that, on the coast and with a view, would sell for at least $100,000. This one had plenty of privacy. It had no next-door neighbor. Your front door was the ocean.

Back then the coast was hardly developed at all. There wasn't a Salishan, the five-star coast resort hotel, and many of the bigger motels hadn't been built. There were only small motels and quaint overnight rest stops—nothing fancy.

I remember driving down the Columbia River on old Highway 30 to Astoria and wondering why there wasn't a bridge connecting Astoria with Washington state. There were ferry boats to carry cars and people across the river. But a bridge was needed.

One fellow I met, a state senator from Astoria named Bill Holmstrom, said that someday there would be a bridge across the Columbia between Astoria and Megler, Washington. People thought he was crazy at the time. But Old Bill fought hard for that bridge and finally, after some years, he got it. I still think they should name that bridge after him.

In the days before the bridge was built, the only excitement in Astoria was looking at the fishing fleet, climbing the Astoria Column, visiting the John Jacob Astor Hotel, visiting a few bakery shops, and seeing the old canneries. At that time there were few restaurants, far fewer than there are today, and logging and fishing were the main industries.

South of Astoria, Seaside was still a small sleepy town. Occasionally on summer holidays the school kids would come and raise hell. Once, back when U.S. Senator Mark Hatfield was governor, the school kids created quite a disturbance. They had to call in the state police, and some of Hatfield's aides had to go down there to calm things down.

But Seaside was basically a quiet and safe little town. You could always get a room, particularly on the winter weekends. There were private houses on the boardwalk and hardly any first-rate motels or other lodging.

The first big nightclub on the coast in the late '50s was Pantley's Pagan Hut at Depoe Bay. It turned out to be the trendy place for Portlanders who wanted to escape from the city and have "fun" without running into anyone they knew, namely friends, wives, or husbands.

But soon everyone was going there and it no longer became an escape. During its heyday Pantley's Hut was the place to let your hair down. Unfortunately, it was right across from the cove and the Anderson cabins, our retreat. The "party" at Pantley's Hut went on until early morning. Eventually we had to find another spot for our weekends.

We used to drive back from the coast along the Wilson River highway. The countryside was quiet then, and there were not many cars. The land was thickly forested with cedar, fir, and hemlock.

I felt free. We all felt free. Somehow the trees and the forests just made us feel free, clean, and healthy. There was no graffiti, no litter along the roadside, no billboards. Everyone seemed to be having a good time enjoying the countryside. People didn't hesitate to park along the roadside and have a snack, or let the kids splash in the mountain stream that meandered nearby.

Sometimes we went down to Newberg and McMinnville in the Salem area. The countryside was always green. There were sheep and field crops throughout that part of the valley. There were no vineyards lacing the hillsides as you see today. No one thought that wine of the quality grown in California could ever be produced here. Not warm enough, they said. And it rained too much.

Today everyone knows that Oregon is a producer of premium wines. It isn't a large producer, but it is recognized for making the finest Pinot Noir. More on that later in this book.

Another of our trips took us through southern Oregon for the first time, on Highway 99W. The freeway had not been completed then, in the late 1950s. Getting to Medford took about 10 hours. From Roseburg south the scenery reminded me of the northern California Sierra Nevada, much drier than northern Oregon and not as green.

Roseburg then was known as the "banana belt" because it was so sunny and warm. The first wine vineyards of any consequence were started there. The climate was similar to the climate in southern France.

Traveling even further south, toward Medford, we always enjoyed the drive along the Rogue River. Even though the road swung and swayed its way between the river and the hillside, you always had a good view of the Rogue, Oregon's famous steelhead trout stream.

Seeing the Rogue always reminds me of my father-in-law, Henry Gault, who was a master fisherman. He lived in Medford, and when I was visiting, he would go out early in the morning and fish the Rogue, returning always about 7 a.m. with his pouch filled with steelhead, ready for breakfast.

I didn't know then that a steelhead trout was a prize game fish. To an easterner like me, trout was just plain trout. But when my mother-in-law first prepared those steelhead trout for me, along with bacon, home fries, and eggs, I tasted a breakfast that hasn't been equaled since. Even today, whenever I drive along the Rogue River or through Medford, I smell bacon and steelhead cooking.

Ginger Rogers, the dancing partner of Fred Astaire, had a ranch on the Rogue and lived there with her mother. It was at her ranch, with her permission, that my father-in-law did his trout fishing. The river attracted other Hollywood stars as well. Clark Gable fished the Rogue many times. The western writer, Zane Grey, also spent many years there. They all loved the Rogue.

Medford in those days had a population of 10,000. The biggest industry was pears. There also was lumber, but the city was most famous for its Rogue River pears.

Medford didn't have as much smog then as it does today, but whenever they smudged the orchards to protect the blossoms from frost, the smog index rose. Medford is in a valley where smog does develop.

Despite that, it was a beautiful small town of old families who had been there for generations. There were few outsiders. Unfortunately, it also had a reputation for being "all white."

A sad chapter in the town's history involves the famous singer Marian Anderson, who was the first black woman to sing for the Metropolitan Opera. She was refused a room in the city's only hotel. To avoid further embarrassment, her hosts, one of the leading families at the time, invited her to stay at their home. Ironically, Anderson returned to Oregon in 1992 to live, occupying one of the most prestigious highrise condominiums in downtown Portland. She came here because of her nephew, James DePreist, conductor of the Oregon Symphony. She died shortly thereafter.

Medford today is different. The California migration has made it so. Neighboring Ashland has helped, too, by bringing people from all over the world to its Shakespeare Festival, and tourists also come to enjoy the beauty of the Rogue River Valley, of which Medford is the capital.

Many Californians are now moving to Ashland and Medford, and the real estate values in these cities are some of the highest in the state. The area still remains one of the state's truly scenic treasures, but I will always remember Medford as it was then, before the freeway bisected the heart of the downtown, destroying the tidy small homes with their proud yards of flowers and vegetables.

Crater Lake was yet another destination for our weekend trips. The beauty of Crater Lake began with the eruption of Mt. Mazama almost 7,000 years ago. After centuries of rain and snow, the crater was filled, creating a pure blue body of water almost 2,000 feet deep—the deepest lake in the country.

Crater Lake Park is largely snowbound most of the year. Even in the height of summer there can be a freak snowstorm. The lake is over 6,000 feet above sea level.

Still another area that we eventually came to explore was southeastern Oregon, the high desert country. The high desert is a land of sagebrush and big sky and large ranches. Residents here are independent and strong like the early pioneers. Yet they are, by far, the friendliest people in the state.

In this part of Oregon is Jordan Valley, the home territory of the Basques. When I first came to Oregon I had no idea who the Basques were. I later found out that they were sheepherders, the best, and that they came from the Pyrenees on the border of southern France and Spain.

Today, the Basque community is still prominent in that part of the state, spilling over into Idaho. The Basques are an energetic, productive, and industrious people. One of the leading state senators in Oregon during the 1950s was a Basque from Jordan Valley, Senator Anthony Yturri. So was one of our leading bankers in Oregon, John Elorriaga.

Jordan Valley is a quiet community that has struck a balance between maintaining its culture and assimilating itself to mainstream American life. There will be more on the Basques later in this book.

Oregon is changing—slowly, and in a way that still offers pleasure to the people who live here. I have a fear, though, that if it changes too fast and tries to copy other states we may lose the magic which existed when I came.

Things have to change, and if that's the way it is going to be, there isn't much we can do about it, except ensure that the changes benefit the majority of the people and give people pleasure in what nature has provided for us.

To many outsiders, Oregon is a land of tall trees and loggers and Pacific salmon and that's about it. It is a state that until recently got very little attention from those who lived in the East or Midwest or even as close as California.

Oregonians, of course, liked it this way because they wanted to keep the secret of Oregon to themselves. A Portland "booster" group that called itself the "Rainmakers" used to give small bottles of Oregon rainwater to visitors. It was intended as a joke, a message to discourage any visitor from moving here. Then there was the James G. Blaine Society, which upheld the importance of being an Oregon native. And one governor, Tom McCall, became celebrated for his infamous statement, "Come visit, but don't stay." That statement has come back to haunt all Oregonians. But McCall was only reflecting the sentiment of his constituency. He was too smart a politician to walk the plank alone.

Today the secret of Oregon is out, revealed by the media. Many people traveling through our state are discovering its beauty.

Now, let me take you through some of the old and some of the new Oregon. Let me show you how Oregon has changed, and let me show you some of the interesting features which continue to attract people to Oregon as they attracted me when I first came.

Let me show you how Oregon takes newcomers, quietly reveals its magic to them, and in doing so, creates new Oregonians.

The Umatillas

Guardians of a sacred legacy

Visiting a reservation may give a non-Indian some sense of uneasiness. I felt that uneasiness when I was about to make my first visit. Maybe it was being reminded of all the hurt of the past that had been suffered by the Indians that gave me a feeling of shame which turned slowly into fear.

Had they forgiven us?

It wasn't easy the first time, and it may not be easy the first time for any white person or Euro-American, as the Indians I met referred to us, to visit a reservation.

When I went to the reservation for the first time, it was to give and to share and not to take. I felt the Native American knew that much more than I did.

Somehow, when you start meeting Indians you feel that many of them have mastered the art of forgiving. They are able to give because they have reached a level of spirituality which they have nourished through a culture thousands of years old.

After visiting not one, not two, but many of our reservations in Oregon, I have many stories to tell about Native Americans, about how they treat their own people and others, and, more important to me and I'm sure to other Oregonians, how they not only respect the earth but revere it.

Native Americans call it Mother Earth. To them Mother Earth came not from other matter but from a creator!

From that spirituality comes a gentleness that is hard for me to describe without becoming maudlin. Here is a story of my first visit to a reservation.

It was dusk, and I had been waiting for Marguerite to come to take me to her office on the reservation. She was to be my host and guide. She met me at Pendleton and then took me over the hill—the "Indian Hills"—to Mission, the home of the Confederated Tribes of the Umatillas. It was only a few miles from Pendleton.

I was tired, also hungry, and wanted to make my visit brief and get back to my motel. I told Marguerite I wanted photographs of some of the young people. I was secretly hoping for an Indian in full regalia, like what you see in the movies or in the picture books. I didn't want to suggest it because I was unsure of the protocol.

As we were driving on the reservation (which looked like any small town with small one-story homes and children's toys scattered about the lawns), I saw him. He was in a truck, a small pickup, and he had shiny black hair braided into a queue. He had a strong face. It reminded me of the face of the Indian on the old nickel.

"Marguerite! Stop! Who was that in the truck? I want his picture." Marguerite, always obliging, honked and the pickup came to a stop. It was a screeching stop.

She motioned to him to follow, and we drove to a spot some hundred yards up the road and then turned into what looked like a recreation and meeting place. We stopped at the longhouse and Marguerite told the driver, whom she obviously knew, to come over. "This is a friend of mine, he wants to take your picture," she announced.

He didn't answer but did come out of his truck. The closer he came toward me, the taller he got. He must have been 6 foot 6 or taller, or so it seemed. I'm only 5 foot 6, and I felt I had shrunk even smaller. He didn't shake my hand, but placed his huge hand under my elbow and gently drew me closer to him. We had not exchanged greetings. He then pointed to the large eastern Oregon moon, which that evening was resting against a deep blue sky filled with a million tiny stars.

"See that moon?" His voice was surprisingly soft, almost reverent. "Yes, I see that moon." I was uneasy and tried to conceal it. To myself, I added, "And anything else you want me to see, I will gladly see."

He looked strong but I was able to see a gentle smile coming from his dark brown eyes. "You see the man in the moon?" he said.

"Of course, who hasn't heard of the man in the moon." My voice was just a little unsteady as I stood close to him, staring at the moon but wanting to turn my attention elsewhere.

"That man in the moon—you see. His head is leaning forward and there are things hanging from his hair," he continued, still holding me close to him.

"Yes," I answered. "I see. I really see." Actually, I saw what I always see—areas that are light and areas that are shaded, but that have no specific shape and don't resemble anything.

I didn't want any confrontation. I was tired and he looked big, very big.

"You know," he went on, "Those things hanging from his head. They are feathers. You see, the man in the moon is an Indian."

I smiled, relieved. But then a strange thing happened. I felt a lump growing in my throat and my eyes suddenly became moist. This surprised me, because I'm not much for public display of sentiment. I looked at him and what I had imagined earlier to have been a mean face suddenly changed to a face wearing an impish grin. I had been found out in my sudden rush of emotion.

I have told that story many times. I will tell it many more times, for each time I tell it, it recalls all the false information I'd been given in the past about supposedly "bad" Indians, information foisted on a too-gullible big-city boy by poorly informed or prejudiced non-Indians.

* * *

To further understand Indians, you must first try to examine their culture, which is revealed to a degree if you go to Pow Wows and visit their reservations.

In recent years the confederated tribes of Native Americans in Oregon and neighboring states have celebrated their origins with festivals or Pow Wows. These Pow Wows are a time to share roots that connect with other tribes and with the Native Americans along our coast, in the Oregon inland mountains and even in the far reaches of the Alaskan tundra. All are welcomed to the Pow Wows—those of Indian ancestry, those whose ancestors forged new trails with oxen, mules, and Conestogas, those who have come to our state only to visit and not to stay. The Pow Wows, once called feather dances, are sort of an annual reunion so people can get together, a family affair where there is food—salmon and fry bread—and dancing and the sharing of stories of past generations. They are held in July and August.

The Pow Wow to the Indian is also the proud wearing of garments of deer skins and of beads and feathers. It is the Circle of Friendship where all face each other in a wide circle made up of all who have come—a circle within a circle, moving in counter-rotation so all can greet each one with a smile and an extended hand. This is Oregon, not only for its Native Americans but for everyone, for everyone is welcomed.

Before you journey to the Pow Wow, here are some memorable words to think about, written by a member of the Confederated Tribes of the Siletz in a brochure to announce the celebration of the Pow Wow. They reveal the people and their relationship to the land, a land they hold sacred. They begin:

The names our fathers and mothers called themselves, like the old ways and like the land itself, were disturbed by Euro-American intrusion in the 1800's.

We call ourselves Siletz Indians today because it is our official name and a name of modern unity, but most of us remember older names that came before confederations. Names such as Chetco, Tootootoney, Yahshute, Eukiechee, Sixes, Joshua, Galleace, Mackanotin, Whiston, Shasta Costa and others that approximate the names that our ancestors gave themselves.

Some of our elders still speak the tongues of their fathers and mothers, but sadly, most members today speak only English.

Gone are the cedar plank houses and the racks of drying salmon.

Many of us live in the town of Siletz, named after the river, Siletz, meaning "twisted" as a snake or rope. Here was the site of the federal agency, "Government Hill," on the reservation.

Nearby is the land that we still own in common, 3,628 acres of timber tracts that are the remnants of the once vast Coast reserve.

For the many more of us who live outside of the Siletz area, Government Hill in the town of Siletz is the place we come each August to visit family and friends at the annual "Nesika Illahee Pow Wow." We come to Government Hill for the Memorial Day ceremonies held at Paul Washington Cemetery, and the bones of our ancestors remind us of our proud past.

We come for Restoration Day in November, and the new Community Center makes us proud today of a strong tribe working to make Siletz home again for us and our children.

When you visit the Pow Wow and talk to the Indians and see their homes and listen as they talk to each other, you will hear from some about the way it is today and from others—the elders—about how it was then. You may hear or even see names that are familiar to you—names such as Rogue, Sixes, Coquille, Coos, Yaquina, and even Siletz and Siuslaw. These may be river names or names of some of our forests. To the Indians the names are their history, their ancestry, names that go back many, many years, even centuries.

Among the Indians, there was diversity not only in names but also in languages. Along our coast among the Confederated Tribes of the Siletz were languages such as Yakonan, Siuslawan, Kusan, Hokan, Coast Salish, and Athapascan.

Again, from the same brochure:

Theirs was a communal life with a world view and a view of self that we today have only a fractured view of. For with the Euro-American invasion came a sudden and shattering breaking apart of the subtle and intricate ties between people, land and other people.

The Pow Wows today try to restore that subtle link between people, land and other people.

For the descendants of the Indians who live with us, there is a growing sense of renewal. You can feel it.

The Indians in Oregon go back to the time before Christ. Along the banks of the Nehalem, Tillamook, Nestucca, and Salmon Rivers, for instance, were settlements of Oregon coastal Indians that date back some 2,500 years. These settlements had a fully developed fishing culture. Their culture was similar to that of the earliest occupants of the Great Basin cultures across the mountains of southeastern Oregon and Nevada.

Today there is an excitement among our Native Americans. There is growth in population and a steady growth in their economy. There is also a defined culture in renaissance which attracts many of them back to the reservation.

The Indian is proud again. And today the Indian wants to share that feeling. Each year, as the spring rains diminish into the dawn of summer, Indian tribes throughout Oregon prepare for the festivals, a time to remember ancestry and celebrate the restoration and strengthening of their tribes.

One of the most recently restored tribes, the Coquilles on the southern Oregon coast, celebrated with a massive salmon bake. It was a proud day— July 1, 1990—when Chief Tony Tanner, just turned 80, celebrated the one-year anniversary of the restoration of the Coquille land.

He could remember that sad day in 1954 when the federal government revoked the tribal standing and its members were told they weren't Indians anymore. They were U.S. citizens regardless of their heritage and distinctly Indian features.

Chief Tony Tanner worked years as a logger but continued with members of his tribe to seek restoration of their tribal rights. It finally came with the passage of the Restoration Act.

They are Indians once again. They know that on this ground lived their ancestors. Only recently, evidence was unearthed—a hearth was discovered that dates back to 200 A.D. Other ancient Indian camps were found near Myrtle Point and Powers, across the Coquille River at Bandon, and at Camas Valley.

The Native Americans in Oregon (and elsewhere) whose tribes have received federal recognition are grateful because with the renewed recognition come federal programs to help the sick, the children, and the hungry. They are also glad for the return of the timber tracts. But more important to the Native American is the gratitude they give their elders. For it was the elders of the tribes who fought for restoration and who did not forget their fathers and their mothers and those who had worked tirelessly to make the Indians' proud past a proud future for their children.

Today, on many of our restored reservations, the tribes manage their resources to provide opportunities in education, health, housing, human services, and other functions of a sovereign Indian nation. Several times each year, the members of the specific tribes gather together as a general council to listen and to speak about tribal needs and ideals. It is a time to plan and prepare for their future and for the future of their children, and it is also a time to reflect on the freshness of the air and to appreciate the quiet solitude of their Native American space. And it is to this grand history, to this serenity of their sacred lands, that the Native American invites all to come and express joy at the annual Pow Wows.

Native Americans, however, still remember the hurt of the past, the turmoil and the tragedy of being ravaged and uprooted and confined. That was the past, not to be forgotten but to serve as a source of strength to heal and to forgive. As the healing goes on, so does the restoring of their ties to the tribes.

* * *

I was able to obtain a greater understanding of Indian ways at a rare and deeply impressive ceremony—the installation of a tribal chief. The Indians at Umatilla call it a "stand-up" ceremony. Only Indians are invited, with few exceptions.

I was one of only seven non-Indians who witnessed in 1990 the "stand-up" ceremony of Chief Carl Donald Sampson, hereditary chief of the Walla Walla tribe. He took the Indian name of PeoPeoMoxMox, or Yellow Bird—the same name as the revered head chief of the Walla Walla people from 1835 to the day he fell mortally wounded on December 7, 1855, at the hands of an Oregon Volunteer.

The tragic end of the reign of PeoPeoMoxMox was intoned in the ceremony of the new chief of the Walla Wallas. What happened to the chief was related to all those at the ceremony by former Chief Grant Wahenaka of Warm Springs and, as it probably has through the years, by the elders of the tribe.

Chief Wahenaka spoke eloquently but simply. His manner of speaking introduced to me a kind of oratory that I had not heard before.

The air was very hot on this day. The temperature had reached 105 degrees by late morning.

The Nichtyoway longhouse on the Umatilla reservation at Mission was filled. It was Saturday morning, July 20, 1990. There were Indians there from the Columbia River tribes. They included the Cayuse, the Celilos, the Umatillas, and others who over the centuries have made the Columbia Basin their home.

* * *

Three times Armand Minthorn, a member of a neighboring tribe, stood, took up his drum, and struck 50 beats to sound the preparation of the ceremony. He spoke first in his native Indian language, then in English. He was introducing the ceremony which was about to begin.

On the south side of the longhouse, seated in bleacher-type seats, were all the women of the representative tribes, including the wife of the new chief, Arleta Sampson. Directly across, facing the long rows of seated women, were the elders, young men, and young boys of the tribes.

"Today, all of us come here to witness a big thing. We gather here to pray for what is to happen, for what is to come out," began Armand Minthorn. He was standing behind the two chiefs, Grant Wahenaka and the new chief, Carl Sampson.

Today, we come here in this longhouse with an open heart and open mind. Tradition guides us and the land provides for us. Today, our creator and this land listen to what we have in our minds and in our hearts.

We ask our creator that our children will have a big memory so they can carry on. Today, we ask our creator to shine a big light in this house. We ask guidance for ourselves through this belief—it is truly a wonderful belief—it has truly helped us all. And we ask our creator to give guidance to this man.

With drumming, song, and ringing of a bell, three native songs soon were sung by all the people. Afterward, the men led the people outside to circle the longhouse, and as they exited each turned a complete circle in a gesture of reverence. The women followed the men, and soon all were outside, circling the longhouse.

The hot July sun scorched the marchers but they moved slowly, reverently, and deliberately nevertheless. It was a procession with all the dignity befitting the high office of chief.

The building was slowly emptied or cleansed, signifying a ritual spiritual cleansing and opening of the ceremony.

After all were seated again inside, Grant Wahenaka came to the center, standing near a dark red woolen blanket and tanned deerskin. Chief Sampson stood beside him, his moccasined feet standing on the deerskin.

There was a moment of contemplation. They stood near a plot of uncovered earth. It had been sprinkled earlier with water, "given a drink," our Indian guide told me. Implanted in the earth was a felt-covered pole on which rested a war bonnet. It was the one to be worn by the new chief.

Grant Wahenaka spoke. "Today we come to the crossroads for our tribes. We all recognize this person as a direct descendant of all the chiefs."

And the chief of the Warm Springs tribe continued in a delivery that made each word strong. Despite his advanced age, his voice had a rich resonant sound. He made you want to listen. His voice was steady, unwavering.

He did not use his arms for effect. In fact, they remained at his side. He did not have to raise or lower his voice either to make an impact or to get people's attention because for the people there, what he said was more important than how he said it.

He talked about traditions of the tribe, tribal history, which included the past chiefs, and the qualifications of the new chief. He began with the story of the death of the first PeoPeoMoxMox. He could not relate the entire story because of the time limitation on the ceremony and the heat. These are the circumstances surrounding the death of that great chief.

According to the historical version related by the Walla Walla tribe, PeoPeoMoxMox was saddened when he heard of the U.S. government's reservation policy. Speaking in council on June 7, 1856, he said that when he first heard of the reservation policy his "heart cried" and that he felt "blown away like a feather." He thought that the whites should be free to travel through his country but that they should not build houses on Walla Walla land.

By the terms of the treaty of 1855, the Nez Perce and the Yakimas (other Indian tribes in the area) were to have a reservation each, while the Cayuse, the Umatillas, and the Walla Wallas were to be placed on a single reservation. Seemingly, PeoPeoMoxMox finally decided to sign the treaty and induced Kamiakan, chief of the Umatillas, to do likewise. According to the Indian reports, on the evening of June 9, 1855, the two chiefs signed the treaty.

Six months later, PeoPeoMoxMox was killed in a skirmish with members of the Oregon Volunteers while trying to wrest a gun from one of the militiamen. A bizarre twist to the story, and one which is seldom related, was that as the chief lay mortally wounded, the regimental surgeon, Dr. Shaw, cut off the ears of PeoPeoMoxMox. They were preserved in a jar of alcohol and were on exhibition in Salem, the Oregon territorial capital, for several years. The great chief was buried 2.5 miles west of the Whitman Mission site.

Within one lifetime, the Walla Walla tribe was reduced from a free to a subjugated people, having to exchange one way of life for another. The sorrow and tribulations that the generation of reservation Indians then had to go through cannot be fully fathomed by anyone who has not had to give up his culture for a quite different culture. In addition, Indians had to deal with general nonacceptance by white Americans, the poor economic situation existing on the reservation at the time, and more or less dishonest Indian agents. They also had to wait for decades for the federal government to fulfill the 1855 treaty obligations.

Chief Wahenaka, in conclusion, recounted the names of the succeeding chiefs after the death of PeoPeoMoxMox and brought the history up to the point where Carl Sampson was asked to be chief and accepted.

"I will accept with pride and humility to serve my people," he said.

And we are here today to recognize PeoPeoMoxMox—that is the name given to Carl as the new chief of the Walla Walla tribe as he has taken the name of his great grandfather.

Before I place the symbol of chieftainship—the feathers of the eagle—I want to say that the eagle was accepted and adopted as a symbol by the American natives long before the federal government ever adopted it as one of its symbols.

The reason for adoption of the eagle as a symbol by the natives was because the eagle was a bird known to be wise, it stood as a symbol of integrity, it stood as a symbol of bravery, it stood as a symbol of freedom, and it stood as a symbol of love.

These are some of the reasons the American natives adopted the eagle as their symbol. So, with the wearing of the feathers of the eagle, a chief gains the wisdom, the knowledge, and the love for his people.

With these words, Chief Wahenaka turned to Carl Sampson, who responded:

My heart, my heart is open to my people—my heart is open to all of you, to what is there, to what is to come, to what has taken place in the past. With the people I stand up today for PeoPeoMoxMox, Homily, Jim Kanine, Jack Abraham.

All these were relatives to my mother, my aunt. Today I give special thanks to the people to have the faith to stand here. To my aunt, to all. Today, this special day, is dedicated to all these elders, to all my aunts who helped me years ago and have gone on to a better place, to a place where we will all join them on one of these days.

Today, they are watching us, watching what we are saying, what we are doing. . . . My heart, my heart cries for what takes place on what we call this special earth, this mother of ours. Of the way we are treating her, by the way we are poisoning her with different dioxins in the water, with different poisons in the air. We are slowly but surely hurting all these things which are dear to our people.

There won't be a legacy for the young ones if we don't stand up now and protect what we have left. There won't be a tomorrow for the sunshine to come up.

There is a saying, I read: "You can dam up the rivers until the waters don't flow, you can pave over the ground so the grass don't grow, but you can't keep that sun from coming up or going down."

And with that, Chief Sampson PeoPeoMoxMox concluded his "stand-up" talk to his people—warning them, alerting them, and then comforting them over the environmental injuries to their mother earth.

This chapter is an insight into our Native American neighbors, those from whom we have borrowed their land, worked it, and earned our living off it, and to whom we are now returning part of it with the hope they will forgive, maybe not forget, the injuries of the past. This small look into our Native American culture may give us a better understanding of who our Native American neighbors are and also reassure all of us of the genuine nature of their open invitation to visit their reservations and share in the circle of friendship at the Pow Wows.

An invitation to a reservation can be arranged by contacting the tribal offices.

The Basques

*Descendants of an
ancient people, leaving
their marks today*

The fact about the Basques in Oregon is: They do exist. This may come as a surprise to many newcomers.

I first entered Basque country just after Easter when the apple and cherry trees were blossoming up and down the Willamette Valley. I was barely into my new assignment as farm editor for *The Oregonian* newspaper when I was lured east of the mountains. It was far east, where the river bordering Oregon and Idaho flows like a shapely snake.

To reach this country from Portland, you can take the beautiful drive through the Willamette National Forest, which extends from the Columbia River south to the Winema National Forest, all territory that is part of the Cascade Range. Any of the highways from Portland or Salem or Eugene heading eastward will lead to the Malheur country. Here the land renounces its heritage of green and offers the high desert, where the sky and earth meet in an amiable union. Lava beds and old craters are monuments to a geological past that can only astonish the modern traveler.

This is Basque country, where Highway 78 ends at Burns Junction and splinters to the east and south on Highway 95. To the east on 95 is Jordan Valley, the settled location of Oregon's main Basque population.

The Basques are the oldest European culture, dating back 12,000 years. Archeologists have said they are a mysterious people and quite impossible to place in a historical context. The Basque language is unrelated to any other tongue in the world.

Part of the confusion surrounding the Basques is the political division of their homeland. Basque country straddles the crest of the western Pyrenees between France and Spain and is divided into seven provinces: three in France and four in Spain. The Basque capital is Vitoria.

Because Basques have been mobile, their culture and life style have not been a mystery. While nearly three million Basques live in the valleys of Euskadi, the Basque country in the Pyrenees, thousands have migrated to Australia, South America, and the U.S.

The Basque presence has been chronicled in the U.S. from the arrival of Columbus in the New World five centuries ago to the California Gold Rush in the last century. Most of Columbus' crew were Spanish Basques.

On arrival in the U.S., the Basques found sheepherding jobs and accepted other menial work to compensate for their lack of English. However, their eagerness for work and advancement allowed them to assimilate into American society, and soon they began holding influential positions in almost every industry.

Idaho is home to one of the largest colonies of Basques in the world outside their homeland. More than 15,000 Basques live there. But the Basques are not only in Idaho; they are also in Oregon, California, and Nevada. They came to Oregon early as sheepherders, and Jordan Valley in Malheur County was the main place they settled. Today, many also live in nearby Ontario and in Burns, in neighboring Harney County. Most of the Basques in Oregon, Idaho, and neighboring states are from Viz Caya in Spain or, as the Basque refer to it, Bizkaia, along the Bay of Biscay.

Boardinghouses run by Basques and serving Basque food were at one time common in Malheur County. The food was hearty and the red wine flowed generously with every meal. There were soups and broth served with vermicelli, salads with fresh vegetables, olive oil, garbanzo beans, and always fish—to the Basque, fish is a necessity. Cod was favored. The meat dish usually was beef or tripe in tomato sauce blended with a chicken base.

Chorizo, a Basque sausage made of pork cured for several days with a sauce, was a favorite. These sausages were made each fall, in quantities to last through the season. Everyone helped: family, boarders, and friends. One person would keep the knives sharpened, and the others would take places in the assembly line to stuff the pig casings or to hang the finished sausage to dry.

Younger members of the family were allowed to make the desserts for boardinghouse guests. Such desserts included apples and pears cooked in wine, puddings, and simple cakes and cookies.

These customs were passed on from generation to generation.

Picnics or festivals are regularly held by Basques to celebrate their culture and traditional way of life. At these colorful gatherings, costumed dancers, weightlifters, singers, and ethnic foods help Basques relive the past and provide memories of a colorful history.

Many of the Basque celebrations are private. But some, like the "Jaialdi," held in Boise in 1990 and 1987, are public.

In 1990, Dick Cockle, a correspondent for *The Oregonian*, wrote about the Jaialdi:

> When thousands of Basques from Spain, Mexico, Venezuela and the U.S. gathered at an international festival, the "Jaialdi" in Boise, the aroma of Basque food mingled with the rough consonants of Euzkera, the Basque language.
>
> It was a festival that brought an estimated 25,000 people to Boise, and to the Basques of Oregon, it was the biggest of festivals.

Another, smaller festival is held on the last weekend every July in Boise, when the Basques gather together for two days of dancing, food, picnicking, and play.

Jordan Valley in Oregon is a sociable community, as are Ontario and Burns. The people are friendly, and one could easily fall into intimate conversation with them, as I did many years ago when I was a visitor at the home of Anthony Yturri, former Oregon state senator.

I also remember well the powerful Oregon banker and chairman of U.S. Bank Corp, John Elorriaga, a Basque from Jordan Valley, who made things much easier for me when I needed financial direction. As a writer and journalist, I have come to recognize that the least of my attributes is a realistic sense of financial planning. Elorriaga showed me not only his professional side but his role as a caring and proud parent. The strong parental feelings of the Basque were evident, and were something we could share equally.

Here are some ways you can visit or study Basque culture.

The major source for a background in Basque culture is the Basque Center and Museum in Boise, about an hour's drive from Ontario, Oregon. The summer schedule begins May 1 to September 30, Tuesdays through Saturdays. The winter schedule begins October 1 through April 30, Thursdays through Saturdays.

The Basques are linked culturally and socially through the North American Basque Organization, or NABO, headquartered in Reno. Each year, many of the NABO chapters in Oregon, Nevada, California, and Idaho hold picnics and other summer activities. The public is invited to some of these.

In Oregon, the first stop for seekers after Basque culture should be Jordan Valley, the prominent birthplace of the Oregon Basque.

On Highway 97, across from the Telleria Market in Jordan Valley, is a jai alai (pronounced "hi li") or handball court (*frontone* in Basque). It was created in 1915 by Ambrosio Elorriaga. It is not used today, but it remains an attraction to Basques who have moved away and who return occasionally to Jordan Valley to visit the land of their immigrant forefathers. Hopefully, it will one day be established as a historic landmark.

Jai alai (a name meaning "celebration") is the game from which handball evolved. It is played with a curved basket (*cesta*) fastened to the arms for catching the ball and hurling it against the wall. The game is popular in Latin America. It is believed that the Basque also invented what we know as paddleball or racquetball. They call it *pala*.

Here is the text of a story published May 23, 1971, on the Basque heritage, and written by Floyd Acarregui for the *Northwest* magazine of *The Oregonian* when I was its editor:

> It is difficult for an individual to express the feelings of a group as one's feelings are largely the sum of one's heritage and experiences. Therefore, no two people are able to express themselves and fully agree even in part on such a vast subject. However, in retrospect, it is easy for us to discern some of the outstanding characteristics of the Basque people, which in large measure influenced our thinking and conduct. Since it is difficult to understand any group of people without an insight into their home and family life, let us open the door to other homes.
>
> The Basque family is a close unit. The family group was never developed by our parents with the theory of being pals to us. Instead, there was a fierce pride in the family name, pride in the accomplishments of any member of the family, the pride of the family standing within the community. For any out-of-the-way acts that member might have committed, the Basque descriptive word "Escandalue" (scandal) was always near the surface.
>
> The undisputed head of the family was always the father. We suspected some behind the scenes encounters between our parents, and

sometimes it flared into the open. But never with the intent of usurping father's place within the family. Our mother's philosophy was always that if the head of the family was in good health and doing well, the family likewise would fare well.

Therefore, the preferred position within the family was Father's. Although our fathers were rather easy going, ambitious and demanding of respect from us, we weren't ruled with an iron hand. We had considerable liberty, but we were well aware of our bounds. They well knew that we weren't always within the prescribed limits, but they didn't embrace the philosophy that "if you are doing something behind our backs, you might as well do it in our presence."

There was no open condoning of unapproved actions and the family respect had to be maintained.

Within a Basque family, many of our present freedoms could not have existed as they would feel the time for the "paulue" (the stick) was long overdue!

The desire to succeed and do well was a strong characteristic of the group.

The Basques were often referred to as being stubborn and hard-headed, but these qualities were very necessary if they were to continue their tasks. Their achievements and associations with sheep business confirms these qualities. They immigrated from northern Spain, a small crowded and rolling section. They had no experience with sheep, but once the Basque devoted himself to this industry which demanded privations and hardships to which they weren't accustomed, there was nothing to do but persevere.

During my father's time, the economy was at a low ebb and as sheep operators were usually in trouble, the banks often sold or transferred bands with very little down payment. Such an opportunity and the confidence the banker displayed weren't to be taken lightly.

The Basques feel that everyone should do whatever he is able to do without regard to the type of labor. Even in dire need, their pride seldom permitted any hand-outs.

As most Latins, the Basque had what amounted to a double moral standard. It wasn't too bad for a young man to seek diversion at out-of-the-way places, but there was no excuse nor reason for a woman to step out of bounds. When such a thing occurred, the stigma lasted to some degree for most of her days! She was referred to as "seltea" or loose. The enforcers of the moral code were our mothers. They had great respect for the human body and at no time was it displayed except in proper attire. We never saw our mothers when they weren't fully clothed. And the only attire our fathers would remove was their shirts—displaying their long undershirt in preparation for the ordeal of shaving with a straight edge razor.

The authority of those in charge was well respected whether it was for the teachers in school or civil authorities. We were never permitted to make derogatory remarks about a teacher at home; they were there to help us—and we were to cooperate fully. Although they had a strong feeling for law and order, prohibition was one law they wouldn't recognize. They referred to this law as one being passed by the women and the churches while the men were off at war!

To them a few drinks of wine with meals was almost as much a part of living as food. Liquor was always on hand for company and although we weren't supposed to use it, it was never out of our reach.

During the depression many of our area, Basques and others, fired stills to provide for the needs of the family.

Our people were all Catholics, but to the consternation of our parish priests, most were anything but practicing Catholics. Many of the men would say they were forced to attend regularly at home and here they would refer to the church as a place for women and children.

Although the men didn't manifest outwardly their beliefs, they were religious and God-fearing.

It wasn't our parents' custom to say grace, but in every home there was a place for the crucifix and the rosary. All Basques demanded their weddings in church. Children were baptized and confirmed in the church and all burials were conducted by the church. The Basque felt these events must be through the church—an absolute must!

The Basques had unusually great zest for spontaneous athletic contests. Anytime two or more of them met, they were contesting in throwing crow bars, or rocks, jumping, lifting weights or playing handball. There were few prearranged events and no costly equipment. They were equally spontaneous with their fun. All that was necessary was an accordion or a guitar player and singing and dancing was under way. They played easily and lively and when it came to having fun, they were second to none. Playing and enjoying their fellow man was an art of our fathers that we are losing rapidly.

In a number of ways our people were like the early pioneers, hard-working, independent, honest and self-reliant. We are told that in many metropolitan areas the ethnic groups are splintering from the American society in protest to modern living, thought and association. This small rural community of Jordan Valley is half Basque or of Basque ancestry and our association with non-Basque has been long and close. In tracing a number of Basque families, half or more of the second generation are married outside their "race!" There can be no splintering in our community as we are a full part of this area.

The melting pot has done its job well. We have our differences within the area but they are never along ethnic lines!

The part our parents and others played in developing this area and our relationships, we consider admirable.

There are a number of utterances outside our community that are alien to our thinking. Whenever we hear of some group's efforts to down-grade the work and accomplishments of the people who developed areas like ours, it doesn't set well. We know well what work and sacrifices the men and women of this rural community and other communities experienced to raise their families. They asked only for the well-being of their families and very little for themselves.

Our mothers would talk about what a wonderful thing it would be to have running hot and cold water on tap—and a bathtub. This was a dream to them. They counseled their family by some of their adages— "it is a sin to ask too many favors from God" or "if you don't appreciate what you have, you have nothing."

Here in Jordan Valley, we have very little if any generation gap. The younger generation doesn't do everything we would like them to— but then we didn't either. However, with our background and country philosophy, we can never accept many of the things which are happening among the younger generation elsewhere. To close this gap, one would have to compromise with principles and that would necessitate being unfaithful to ones self.

In retrospect, we have lived well and enjoyed living in this little community. Our small-school associations were close with memories we still relate and enjoy. Speaking personally, I've felt no stigma in this community or other communities along the coast where I have lived, because I was of Basque descent. I can't say that I haven't been unduly apprehensive, but then, who is so smug in himself that he isn't a little concerned at times? We believe that our families did well to settle in Jordan Valley and to teach us to enjoy this type of rural living.

And now for an added treat, here are some recipes from the home of Mr. and Mrs. Floyd Acarregui that were given to *The Oregonian*'s *Northwest* magazine and also published May 23, 1971.

One of the surprises to me was that the Basques were not total meat-eaters. I had assumed they were because of their association with sheepherding, but an important part of their diet is fish and other non-meat items.

Walking into the kitchen of the Acarregui family was like returning to my own family. The smells of delicious food permeated the air. In minutes I was telling about my mother and her recipes and how I longed for those early days when the sound of my mother cooking and the aroma that came from her kitchen gave me all the happiness that any youngster needed. There is nothing in this world that brings out love and with it security more than a mother preparing, with love, favorite dishes for her family. Cooking for another person is a gesture of love, whether for a friend, a family member, or someone with whom there is a romantic attachment. So it was not difficult for me to see the bonds which existed in the Acarregui family when they told me about their cuisine and then generously shared with me some of their family recipes.

Lambless Favorites

These are some popular Basque dishes, supplied by Mrs. Acarregui:

Tongue

    One beef tongue
¼ cup flour
1 egg beaten with 3 tablespoons of milk
½ cup vegetable oil
1 2 oz. can pimento
1 4 oz. can mushrooms
    Salt and pepper to taste

Cook tongue in pressure cooker about 1 hour or until tender. Trim and remove skin. Cut in 1/4 inch slices. Roll in flour, then in egg mixture and fry in oil. Place in a 10-inch by 6-1/2 inch baking dish. Pour pimentos and mushrooms over tongue. Add salt and pepper. Add enough water to just cover tongue. Bake in slow oven (325 degrees) one hour. Serves six.

Spanish Rice

- 1 slice ham, chopped
- 4 slices bacon, cut up
- 1 clove garlic, minced
- ½ cup chopped onion
- ½ cup chopped green pepper
- 1 small can tomato sauce
- 1½ cups rice
- 3 cups water
- 1 teaspoon salt
- ⅛ teaspoon pepper

Fry bacon and ham in heavy skillet. Add onion, garlic and peppers. Cook until soft, add rice, tomato sauce, water, sugar, salt and pepper. Cook slowly for 45 minutes. Serves six.

Flan

- 6 slightly beaten eggs
- ¾ cup sugar
- ¼ teaspoon salt
- 4 cups scalded milk
- 1 teaspoon vanilla
- ¾ cup sugar (for caramelizing)

Melt sugar to caramelize in a 7×4 inch heavy pan over low heat. Shake pan as sugar melts. Cook until golden brown. Shake around edges. Cool. Combine eggs, sugar and salt. Slowly stir in slightly cooled milk and vanilla. Pour mixture into caramelized sugar in pan. Set in water in shallow pan. Bake in slow oven 325 degrees for at least one hour or until knife inserted in center comes out clean. Serves six.

Mount Hood and Timberline Lodge

An authentic original is snatched back from oblivion

Sean O'Faolain once wrote, "We do not really go to places, we come to them. They, always there, are waiting for us."

To be sure, the mountain reigns over us. It is a powerful and noble attraction.

The Portland skyline is dominated by Mt. Hood to the northeast and Mt. St. Helens to the north. They have been dramatically placed so everyone can see the strength they possess.

Mt. Hood, like Mt. St. Helens, is an active volcano. Mt. St. Helens displayed its force in 1980. Mt. Hood fumes quietly but is not to be ignored.

Visitors come to Mt. Hood not only to ski on its slopes and to hike the trails but to visit and linger awhile in the beautiful Timberline Lodge, built in the early 1930s. This lodge is one of the most important historic landmarks in the state. It has national significance because it is the work of artists and master craftsmen of the Great Depression who were hired by the government to build it, as part of the WPA or Work Projects Administration, a federal program designed to put millions back to work. In 1937 the lodge was dedicated by President Franklin Delano Roosevelt.

The lodge is one of the best examples of Western architecture of the period. It has been described as a living museum of arts and crafts inspired by pioneer, Indian and wildlife themes.

There was a brief period when the lodge was not used. It was closed during the years of World War II. Soon, interest in the lodge faded as Oregonians looked elsewhere for their recreation.

It was not until 1955 that an easterner, Dick Kohnstamm, assessed its potential and, with his wife, Molly, made the bold decision to lease the lodge from the U.S. Forest Service. Kohnstamm reopened the lodge and soon began restoring it. Today, more than one million visitors each year use the hotel accommodations, food service, and year-round skiing facilities.

At Timberline, the art works and ornamentation are not just for show. Visitors are welcomed to use the restored furnishings. There are sturdy wood and wrought-iron couches and chairs. Visitors can read by the light of hand-forged lamps and touch the sculpted animals on hand-carved bannister turns. There are more than 200 pieces of oil paintings, watercolors, and lithographs on exhibit.

The restoration process is ongoing, and Timberline Lodge is always in need of carpenters, cabinetmakers, seamstresses, tile layers, stonemasons, writers, weavers, blacksmiths, photographers, architects, conservators, and rug hookers to apply their skills. Their contributions can preserve the lodge for the future generations to enjoy.

I would not like to see this historic attraction ignored by future generations as it was in the early years of my residence in Oregon. Enjoy Mt. Hood and Timberline Lodge, because few places can provide you with such inexhaustible pleasure.

The Soul Solace of the Monasteries

*Where the sore of heart go
when the world won't go away*

His face had happy lines which showed he had been kind to people. His eyes were blue, a deep blue. They made the sky look pale. When he smiled, I was at ease, and I began to tell him of my pain.

That was many years ago, and since then, and before, many, many people have come to the hill because it draws them there when they are in need of solace.

I will always remember the kindness of this person and how I felt cheated that he could not spend more time with me, just to talk. The more I went to the hill, the less time I had with him. Eventually I realized that Father Bernard Sander, O.S.B., was not ignoring me, but telling me in his own quiet way that I was becoming part of the hill and because of that was to share with others what had been shared with me.

One day he showed me a photograph of himself. He was standing in front of a bay laurel, smiling in a way that all but told you he really wondered why he had been chosen as a model to represent the hill. He looked genuinely shy, and you knew the person who had taken the picture had not made a mistake. But then, Imogen Cunningham, the nationally known portrait photographer, seldom did.

* * *

The hill is where the monks of the Benedictine Order settled when they came to this country from their mother house in Engelberg, Switzerland. It is filled with the stories of many men and women, including Aleksandr Solzhenitsyn, Basil Cardinal Hume of England, Governor Vic Atiyeh of Oregon, and even Duke Ellington, who in 1970 conducted the dedication music for the opening of the abbey library. Both the great and the humble have come here to get away from the maddening pace, to rest, to think, and renew themselves.

* * *

Before the monks came in the late nineteenth century, the hill had a special meaning, not to the farmers of the valley, but to the Native Americans, who considered it a spiritual place.

Eight years before Oregon was made a state, an Indian agent by the name of Timothy Davenport surveyed a butte located at the site of what is now Mount Angel Abbey. According to the research of Benedictine monk Br. Simon Hepner, the Indian agent described the butte as 300 feet high and fringed at its base by fir groves, with a spacious crest devoid of timber.

The agent had observed many semicircular walls of stone, each about four feet high, about as high as one's shoulder when one is in a sitting position. He concluded that the stone structures were used as seats. The seats had been constructed of the loose stone found in plentiful supply on the butte. All of them faced west, overlooking the valley.

The presence of the stone chairs in an area which appeared uninhabitable created for Davenport a small mystery waiting to be solved. He started asking questions of the few settlers in the valley and learned that the Indians had made the stone artifacts. When he described to the Indians the reports given to him by the settlers, they told him that the stone chairs and their use were an inheritance from their ancestors. They were unable to tell him when the first ones were built. But according to their legends, Indians traveling north and south used the Klamath Indian Trail about three miles east of the butte or what is now Mount Angel Abbey. They usually camped upon the banks of the Abiqua Creek. The nearby butte eventually became a sanctuary for them during their journey. They used the stone chairs on the butte as pews for prayer. According to the Indians, they received inspiration, renewed strength, and hope on this mountain, which they called Tap-A-Lam-A-Ho, or Mount of Communion. When Davenport asked them why they spent the time and effort to climb the mountain when they could easily have worshipped in the valley below, they replied that the Great Spirit dwelled near the mountain top.

A slightly different version of the story is told by Robert Horace Down in his book *History of the Silverton Country* (Portland, Berncliff Press, 1926). Down writes that there was a shrine on Tap-A-Lam-A-Ho, and that the Indians made long journeys from the south and east to visit it. Since the hill was close to the Klamath Trail, many stopped there to worship.

The shrine was a small circular enclosure which faced the south side of the hill. From the summit, the Willamette Valley was visible for miles. The small circular enclosure could have been the stone chairs mentioned by Davenport.

As the white migration to the valley increased, the Indians were forced off their land and gradually were denied access to the butte and much of the surrounding territory. The settlers started a town near the butte and called it Roy (later its name was changed to Fillmore). To the local residents the butte became known as Lone Butte Hill or Graves Butte. So it remained until 1881, when it once again became a place of worship.

In that year, according to Br. Hepner, a Benedictine monk, Father Adelhelm Odermott, traveled here from the Engelberg Benedictine Abbey in Switzerland in search of a refuge for the monks of Engelberg. At that time the abbey in Engelberg was considering relocation because its relations with the Swiss government were becoming difficult.

When Father Odermott stopped in Portland, he was asked by the archbishop to take over Sunday services in the small town of Fillmore. While there, he was taken by the townspeople to the top of the butte.

On that hilltop he discovered the ideal site for an abbey. The butte and the surrounding valley reminded him of Engelberg. The archbishop, who earlier had expressed interest in the site for a religious institution, was pleased with the decision by the monks and gave his support. On June 17, 1882, the chapter in Engelberg gave its permission to begin building a sister monastery. (Meanwhile, the mother house remained in Engelberg, riding the tide of discontent with the Swiss government. It is still there today.)

On November 13, 1882, Father Odermott and the few monks who had come here with him began saying their divine offices, or daily prayer. The religious practice continues to this day.

In 1883, the town of Fillmore changed its name to Mount Angel. This is the English translation of Engelberg.

There is no evidence today as to the location of the stone chairs. Some feel they were on the south side of the hill, on the slope that overlooked what later became the abbey athletic field.

The slope was leveled by the monks to make room for the athletic field,

a tennis court, and an indoor swimming pool. For years the tennis court and the pool and athletic field were much used by the monks and their guests.

In my first visits to the abbey in the '60s I had a strange feeling about the tennis courts, the athletic field with its finely groomed cinder track, and the Olympic-sized indoor pool. They seemed out of place in a monastery. As the years passed, I began to notice fewer people on the courts or in the field. One day, after an absence of almost two years, I visited the abbey. The retreat house that overlooked the tennis courts and part of the field had been enlarged, and in the new addition, a chapel had been built for retreatants, where they could sit in silence in a room designed strictly for contemplative prayer.

Outside, in the field below, weeds had overtaken the once carefully groomed athletic field. The cinder track was no longer smooth. On the tennis courts the earth had settled, and fissures had developed to form a bedding for the ever-persistent weeds.

As for the swimming pool? A fire had gutted the pool building one night. For years, it remained a scarred monument to a less dedicated lifestyle. It is no longer in use.

Somehow, something or someone was reclaiming the past of that once-sacred Indian hill that had been bulldozed to make space for the pursuit of more personal and physical needs.

* * *

From the chiming of the bells on the hilltop of Mount Angel Abbey, the monks are being summoned to prayer. It is late afternoon. Vespers. The chanting of the hill's devout is soon drowned out by the winds that frequent the hilltop.

The tall sequoias planted more than four score years ago by a young monk stand firm against the continuous battering of the wind. They are a barrier shielding the monastery church.

Below the winding road, the small merchants of Mount Angel lock their doors and hurry home. Children come in from play, and mothers hasten to prepare yet another activity for the remainder of the day. All seem oblivious to the ritual of the contemplative community which obediently follows the rules set down hundreds of years ago by an Italian monk named Benedict.

Soon vespers will be followed by an hour or so of personal time. Then the monks are summoned again by the sounding of the bells to compline, another set of prayers that prepare the soul and body for a quiet evening of rest.

Mount Angel Abbey is one of several Catholic communities of monastic orders in Oregon that offer a place for the lay person of all denominations to spend quiet time. Here you can retreat from schedules, from the anger of the evening rush hour, from the boredom of routine, and from the neighbor who you find more and more difficult to love because you no longer love yourself.

Below is Father Bernard Sander's definition of a retreat:

Despite the corporate definitions a retreat is a period of seclusion away from the pressures of ordinary life.

The spiritual retreat is a time set apart either by oneself or in company with a group. A spiritual retreat requires that the person go to a special place which is so situated as to give opportunity for quiet reflection and prayer.

Usually the retreatant will seek out some kind of spiritual direction and will spend time away from noise and distraction. The purpose of a spiritual retreat is to help the retreatant come to a close reunion with God and a more understanding relationship with fellow human beings.

* * *

Throughout Oregon, but mostly in the Tualatin and Willamette valleys, communities of nuns and monks have opened their doors to welcome the stranger in need of rest and quiet time.

The Benedictines are the oldest order of monks in the Catholic Church, governed by what they refer to as the Rule of St. Benedict. This is a rule that Benedict wrote for his monks before he died in the fifth century. Benedict wanted to separate himself from the secular concerns of the world outside and establish a self-sufficient economic unit to teach others and help the poor of the world.

Those who follow Benedict's way of Christian life are called Benedictines. The men are monks and live in monasteries. The women, living in priories or convents, are called nuns or sisters.

Although these monks and nuns have retired from the world under religious vows, they invite the world to come and visit and even spend some time with them. They have set aside quarters for visitors where the weary can retreat from the mainstream. These quarters are commonly known as retreat houses. There are persons who come for individual private retreats and many who come with groups. Visitors also are welcome to tour the abbey grounds and join the monks in their worship services.

The Rule of St. Benedict is clear in guiding the monks in their treatment of visitors: "All guests who present themselves are to be welcomed as Christ, for He himself will say: 'I was a stranger and you welcomed me.'" "Proper honor," the rule continues, "must be shown to all."

Historically, the strongest influence in shaping the Christian spirit among the people of East and West during the early ages came from the monasteries. According to J.G.M. Cardinal Willebrands, one of today's leaders in the Catholic Church, "There were great popes, patriarchs and bishops as there were princes, emperors and kings, in both East and West, . . . some of whom rank as saints. But the monks were everywhere, in the towns, in the country. They lived out the ideal of the Christian life among the people. . . . The presence of the monks endured through the wars between the empire and church, through the struggles between popes and emperors and through the barbarian invasions."

Today, the monks, no longer faced with struggles between emperors and popes, offer their way of life as a humbling example for those who are lured by the false security of material things.

* * *

It is not only the Benedictines of Mount Angel who have opened their doors. Others also want to share the enrichment of their lives.

The tiny enclave of monks of the Brigittine Order who have settled near Amity also have room for guests. The Brigittines differ from the Benedictines in that their mission is almost continuous prayer and an almost complete separation from the secular world. They do not leave the abbey, in contrast to the Benedictines, who do because of their educational mission.

The Brigittine Order was founded in 1370 by St. Brigitta (Bridget) of Sweden, and has been in Oregon since 1986. The order has both nuns and monks. In Amity, only monks live at the monastery, known as Our Lady of Consolation.

The Brigittines have built a new church from the sale of confections, the popular chocolate fudge. The fudge and other gourmet sweets, including chocolate truffles, chocolate raspberry truffles, and milk chocolate, have brought this small band of monks national publicity. They have been featured on both national network and cable television.

Despite their exposure, the monks maintain a rigid and deeply religious daily routine. They rise every day at 4:30. They pray eight times a day and attend daily mass.

A gentleness, which to the outsider may be misinterpreted as naiveté, is present in each and every monk of this community. It is this gentleness, however, combined with their love of prayer and work, that makes them excel in what they do.

For these monks, the joy of living together in unity imitates for them the life of Jesus living in the bond of love with his apostles.

* * *

To the north of Amity, over the hill where the land continues rich, is another cloistered community of monks, on the outskirts of Lafayette about five miles northeast of McMinnville.

I remember the late '50s and early '60s, when Oregonians, it seemed, only addressed Oregonians, and the new immigrants to the state had to seek companionship from each other. It was the days of the Bensons and the Unanders, the Johnsons and the Swensens, a time when the McKays talked only to the McKays and when many Oregon governors and other politicians took their cues from the Arlington Club in Portland, the mecca of politics of the day. It was then, isolated from my cultural roots and alone, that I read about a small group of religious men—Trappist monks—who had moved to Oregon from New Mexico—outsiders to Oregon, like myself, who shared my Catholic faith. They had settled north of Amity, years before the Brigittines came, and there they plowed and worked the rich soil of the Chehalem Valley.

These monks were of Benedictine lineage, a reform spin-off seeking a simpler life. They were known as the Trappist Cistercian Order.

To perpetuate their mission, the monks at Lafayette are able to subsist today by also producing food items which in themselves are not essential but do have a market value. They have found a niche in the dessert industry and have become known for their holiday fruit and date-nut cakes. The returns have enabled them to continue their work in helping others.

* * *

It was a blustery day—the kind that autumn unveils in Oregon during the months of October and November. I had little to be excited about. Rain and more rain and then the likelihood of even more presented to me an image of Oregon I didn't want to contemplate.

The telephone on my desk rang, and someone calling himself "Brother Martin" was on the other end. "I read your story in *The Oregonian* about the migrants," he said. "If you ever get by the Trappist Abbey here in Lafayette, drop in and say hello."

I called him several weeks later and told him I would like to visit him. I had no idea what to expect. He did tell me the first time we talked that I could spend the night.

Something was pushing me there. My wife said it would be good for me . . . a weekend of rest. I think she and the children needed the rest from me.

I didn't drive to Lafayette but took the bus and was dropped off at the cafe in the center of town.

He was waiting for me, with a big smile across his dark-complexioned face. He was wearing a pea jacket and a sailor's cap. He certainly didn't look like a monk. He looked like a formidable middleweight boxer who could go a rough ten rounds without enduring even a mark.

Our drive to the Abbey was just about two to three miles.

There was a small guest house with four or five overnight guest rooms, adjoining a slightly larger building that housed a dining area, a visitor's lounge, and a small bookstore. (That was back in the '60s. Today, there are more accommodations for retreatants.)

My first thought was that it would be difficult for me to spend the night there, in a small cell-like room with no one to talk to and only myself to think about. It was a change, but whether it was for the better I couldn't immediately tell. The switch from frantic pace to almost a standstill was a jolt.

However, I found this "middleweight," known affectionately as Br. Martin, to be wise beyond his years. The simplicity of his conversation revealed to me a compassionate, strong man who had endured. Somehow, his kindness and sincerity were soothing, and my anxiety all but faded away. I no longer was intimidated.

There was no lecture, no preaching, no admonishment, no judgment. There was an honesty about this man that revealed the secret of the tranquility which exists at the Trappist community—our Lady of Guadalupe Abbey.

In the years since that first visit, I have returned many times to see and talk with Br. Martin and also others such as Br. Luke and Br. Mark and Father

Pascal, and even the abbot, Bernard McVey, a man of gentility and rare nobility. Abbot Bernard has since retired, turning over the spiritual reins to a much younger monk, Abbot Peter McCarthy.

In my first encounter with the monks living this cloistered life, I wondered whether they were there only for a limited period of time, to return later to the outside world. I found that the life of a monk is not offered on a temporary basis. It is a choice to be made for the remainder of one's life. A monk can always leave. However, if he sought to return, his reacceptance by the community would be rare. The decision to enter a monastery means closing the door to the outside world. The monk has to dedicate his life to prayer and helping others. He has a new family and a new life.

* * *

I also learned more about Our Lady of Guadalupe. For years I had seen the picture in the churches. It was a picture of the Virgin Mary, standing in what appeared to be a huge seashell. This picture, seen in churches all over North America, and particularly where many Catholic Hispanics worship, is a reproduction of what once miraculously appeared on the woven shawl of an illiterate Mexican peasant, Juan Diego, who lived during the time of the conquistadores' rule in Mexico.

In the mid-sixteenth century, on a cold December day, just outside what is now Mexico City, Juan Diego had a vision. He had seen the Mother of Christ, he said, not just once, but three times, and to prove it to the doubting community, the picture of the Virgin Mary had been miraculously painted on his shawl.

In a few years a massive conversion took place. More than one million Indians rejected their ways and became Catholics, hastening the proselyting efforts of the Spanish conquerors. To this day, the shawl of Juan Diego hangs in the Basilica of Our Lady of Guadalupe on the outskirts of Mexico City.

The mystery of the shawl was so enrapturing that I spent several years looking into this story and found it not only intriguing but revealing. I realized what immense faith rests with the Catholics of Mexico. I saw this with my own eyes: Every day at the Basilica of Our Lady of Guadalupe in Mexico thousands go to the shrine, some approaching on their knees, to see the shawl worn by Juan Diego, which bears the image of the mother of Christ imprinted mysteriously almost 500 years ago.

The image is rendered in all three media of paint, and to this day scientists are unable to explain how it was applied or the reason for its lasting this long. A shawl of similar material, which is ordinary sisal hemp, would have disintegrated by now.

The shawl is the center of devotion for the millions of Mexicans and Hispanics throughout North America.

And, at Lafayette, in the small abbey tucked away quietly in the lower foothills of the Chehalem Mountains, just 30 miles southwest of Portland, Trappist monks say their daily prayers to the Lady of Guadalupe, whose image is on a shawl that has been revered and seen not only by millions of Mexicans but by popes and even a U.S. President—John F. Kennedy.

Directory of Oregon Retreat Centers

Alton L. Collins Retreat Center
    32867 SE Highway 211
    Eagle Creek, Oregon 97022
Christian Renewal Center
    22444 North Fork Road SE
    Silverton, Oregon 97381
Franciscan Renewal Center
    0858 SW Palatine Hill Road
    Portland, Oregon 97219
The Grotto
    PO Box 20008
    Portland, Oregon 97220
Loyola Retreat House
    3220 SE 43rd Avenue
    Portland, Oregon 97206
Mount Angel Abbey Retreat House
    St. Benedict, Oregon (Mount Angel) 97373
Our Lady of Peace Retreat
    3600 SW 170th Avenue
    Beaverton, Oregon 97006-5099
St. Benedict Lodge
    Dominican Ret/Conf Ctr.
    56630 N. Bank Rd.
    McKenzie Bridge, Oregon 97401

St. Rita's Retreat Center
    PO Box 310
    Gold Hill, Oregon 97525
Shalom Prayer Center
    840 S. Main Street
    Mt. Angel, Oregon 97362
Tilikum: Ctr for Ret & Outdoor Min.
    15321 NE North Valley Road
    Newberg, Oregon 97132
    (Private and unstructured retreat houses)
Our Lady of Guadalupe Trappist Abbey
    PO Box 97
    Lafayette, Oregon 97127
Brigittine Monastery
    23300 Walker Lane
    Amity, Oregon 97101

Mt. Angel—City of Oktoberfest

Peak excitement near the top of a storied mountain

Of all the cherished memories of my early journeys into the heartlands of the Willamette Valley, that of Mt. Angel stands out the most vividly.

Though I have no blood ties to the predominately German community in Mt. Angel, I do consider it a home away from home. It is the force of the abbey that brings me there. Sometimes my soul is too frail and needs the nourishment of the spiritual life, which is more than abundant on the hill where the abbey is located (see chapter on monasteries).

It has been more than a quarter century since that phone call one morning from a Catholic Benedictine monk, Father Albert Bauman of Mt. Angel Abbey. He wanted me to visit him at Mt. Angel for a meeting with several of the farmers in that community.

They were planning a harvest festival and wanted me to be the first to know since at the time, I was a farm editor of *The Oregonian*. Father Albert had elected to give a helping hand to the farmers, who felt such a festival would bring revenue to the tiny community. The farmers, in turn, had always showed their support for the abbey, which was on the hill at the eastern fringe of town.

Father Albert was a cheerful man who had distinguished himself as a journalist. He was exuberant, and his manner of presenting suggestions always won people over. In my particular case, he wanted me to share in this excitement, and, of course, translate that excitement into a story in the newspaper. Having never heard of an Oktoberfest before, I became enthusiastic after I heard what he envisioned as one of the great ethnic festivals of the future.

The festival was designed to begin in a small way and, hopefully, to grow. That was in the mid-1960s. Today, Mt. Angel is renowned for its festival, held each year beginning always on a Thursday and continuing through Sunday in mid-September.

For the first few years, the festival grew slowly. The monks from the hill gave their support, as did the nearby nuns at the Benedictine Convent south of the town center on Main Street, just west of Highway 214. The original beer garden, or Biergarten, was located in a small lot on Main Street across from the service station and near the old train depot, which later turned into an antique shop. As early as the first festival, German bands filled Mt. Angel's air with oompah polka tunes, and booths offered a cornucopia of ethnic foods: wine, sauerkraut, sausage, and cheese.

Such a festival was always a dream of the early settlers of Mt. Angel, many of whom lived here when it was known as Fillmore and even at one time Roy. The settlers wanted their children to know the customs of their forebears and speak the father tongue, which was Swiss German. They had built sturdy houses and established schools. The pride of the community was St. Mary Church, probably one of the most beautiful churches in Oregon, with a gothic spire rising more than 200 feet above the street, visible for miles in almost all directions. It was damaged in 1993 by a violent earthquake. Rather than build a new church, the parishioners restored the church to its traditional splendor.

Just a few miles from Mt. Angel, in the low foothills of the Cascades, lies the small mission church at Crooked Finger, the Holy Rosary Chapel. The chapel is the scene each year of the Marian Pilgrimages of Crooked Finger, occurring on each of the universal feast days of the Blessed Virgin.

Today, in the center of Mt. Angel, there are hanging flower baskets, 69 of them to be exact, all maintained and freshened daily. Some of the annuals lending their color and adding their charm to this display are lobelias, geraniums, marigolds, petunias, zinnias, and begonias. During the festival the explosion of floral color and sounds of merry-making people, young and old, all become features of this wonderful and exciting party.

In the center of town is the Fruchtsaeule, the harvest monument, symbol of a bountiful harvest.

There are bicycle races, volleyball tournaments, and, of course, one of the favorite German pastimes, volksmarching (walking in groups). Arts and crafts are displayed by artists of varying talents. Alpine booths serve delicious ethnic foods ranging from barbecued chicken to the always-popular traditional sausage.

On the outskirts of the festival grounds is a cavernous hall where bands, beer, and singing combine in a perpetual celebration. Then there is the popular Weingarten, where a selection of German and Oregon wines, plus a "German Bier," are offered in a relaxed atmosphere, for family, both children and adults.

There is even a Kindergarten with magic shows, puppets, and pony and tram rides—all free. A symphony orchestra performs, and the bandstand near City Hall is alive with music, singing, and yodeling.

There are also tours to the Benedictine Sisters Catholic Priory nearby, within walking distance. Buses leave the bandstand often for arranged tours of the Mt. Angel Abbey on the hill.

But be forewarned. You might become obsessed with Mt. Angel, both the town and the abbey, and you might want to become part of their community, for better or for worse. The entire milieu provides a wide range of expressions of what life can and should be.

Covered Bridges

A unique tradition, inspired by the Oregon rain

They always fascinate people. Yet it is not their beauty or elegance that gives covered bridges their fascination. Frankly, as bridges they just fulfill their basic purpose. Their beauty is definitely in the eyes of the beholder. But there is a mystique about covered bridges in Oregon that piqued even my cosmopolitan curiosity.

Historically, covered bridges came about when pioneers decided to cover their bridges from the notorious rainy weather. Practical Oregonians also realized that covering a bridge would increase its life span: I'm told the cover design adds 10 to 30 years. Oregonians built their bridges of the abundant Douglas fir trees, which were felled and hewn right at the bridge sites.

Indeed, these bridges are an important part of our early history. Inspired more by practicality than by artistic considerations, the structures possess a rural soul.

Near Portland, in the Willamette Valley in Linn County, is a collection of covered bridges that dates from the 1930s. There are other covered bridges in Oregon, but Linn County offers a detailed self-tour guide that allows for an easy excursion.

Albany, being the county seat and located on I-5, would like you to think it is the center of covered bridge country. Actually, Scio, a little to the east of Albany, has better claim to the title, with five bridges in close vicinity. There also are bridges near Stayton and Silverton in Marion County, and at Crawfordsville, Sweet Home, and Cascadia, all east of Albany.

From Albany, a two-hour drive can take you past five of the bridges, or you can add a couple of hours and swing south to pick up three more. There is one "ghost bridge" named the Bohemian Hall. As this book went to press, the Bohemian Hall remained in storage at the Linn County Road department near Scio. The Albany Visitors Association was sure it would be located eventually near Albany on Cox Creek, but the Scio Chamber of Commerce seemed just as certain it would wind up in Scio as a bridge for foot and bicycle use.

If you are traveling eastward from Albany, first on Highway 20 and then bearing left on Highway 226, you can encounter six of the northernmost bridges as follows.

Hoffman Bridge (1936), located on Hungry Hill Drive, measures 18 feet by 90 feet. Its characteristic feature is Gothic-style windows. Trees were cut on nearby Hungry Hill and hauled by horses to the construction site for this bridge.

Gilkey Bridge (1939), over Thomas Creek, on Goar Road, is a twin in design to the Weddle Bridge at Sweet Home, although slightly wider, measuring 22 by 120 feet. It features exposed trusses and rounded portals. It once stood next to a covered railroad bridge.

Shimanek Bridge (1966), over Thomas Creek, on Richardson Gap Road, measures 22 by 130 feet. It is the newest, and is unique in Linn County for its red paint, old-style portal design, and louvered windows.

Jordan Bridge (1937), over Salem Canal, measures 18 by 90 feet. Swing north to Stayton to take this one in. It connects Pioneer and Wilderness Parks in Stayton. It also formerly bridged Thomas Creek in Linn County before being moved to Stayton.

Hannah Bridge (1936), over Thomas Creek, on Camp Morrison Drive, measures 20 by 105 feet. Thomas Creek seems to have more than its share of covered bridges. This one comes out of a narrow canyon and features exposed trusses and rounded portals.

Larwood Bridge (1939), over Crabtree Creek, on Fish Hatchery Road, measures 20 by 103 feet and has open trusses. A beautiful forested park, a picnic area, and a fine swimming spot surround the bridge. The old water wheel downstream has been restored and adds to the charm of the area.

Larwood completes the circular swing with Scio as the center. To see the remaining three Linn County bridges, go back to the intersection of Highways 20 and 226 east of Albany and shoot down 20 through Lebanon to Sweet Home.

Weddle Bridge (1937), over Ames Creek, on 14th Avenue, measures 18 feet by 120 feet. Located in Sweet Home's Sankey Park, this bridge features exposed trusses and rounded portals. The bridge carried traffic over Thomas Creek for 43 years until being bypassed in 1980. It was moved to Ames Creek in 1989.

From here, go east to Cascadia to Short Bridge or west on Highway 228 toward Brownsville for the Crawfordsville Bridge.

Short Bridge (1945), over South Santiam River, on High Deck Road, measures 20 by 115 feet, and is one of the few remaining bridges with a shingle roof. It is part of Cascadia State Park, and is primarily used to reach nearby Soda Springs.

Crawfordsville Bridge (1939), over Calapooia River, on Highway 228, measures 20 by 105 feet. It features slit windows on each side and is the oldest of this area's covered bridges. It was bypassed by the highway in 1963 and now stands beside the main road. McKercher Park, an excellent picnic spot, lies one mile downstream.

The "ghost bridge," Bohemian Hall (1947), measures 20 by 120 feet. It originally had wooden trusses housed in sheet metal. It was moved from Crabtree Creek on Richardson Gap Road. Hopefully, it soon will have a useful and picturesque location, if it hasn't been placed in one already.

The other Marion County bridge is Gallon House, on Highway 214 out of Silverton. Built in 1917, it is the only covered bridge still in active use on a main road. It reputedly got its name during Prohibition when it was a drop point for bootleg whiskey between "wet" Mt. Angel to the north and "dry" Silverton to the south.

Lane County, in the Eugene-Springfield area and extending to Florence on the coast, also has a number of covered bridges, 18 in all, 16 of them on its current road system. The Lane County Public Works Department has a complete guide.

The Lane County bridges surround the Eugene-Springfield area on all sides, extending east to Office Bridge at Oakridge, south to Dorena on Government Road, north to Ernest on Paschelke Road, and west to Deadwood on Deadwood Loop.

The Lane County brochure lists them in the following order, starting at the north and moving clockwise, with two privately owned bridges listed last.

- Ernest Bridge (1938), on Paschelke Road, near Marcola
- Wendling Bridge (1938), at Mile Point 3.5, on Wendling Road
- Goodpasture Bridge (1938), visible from the highway on Goodpasture Road
- Belknap Bridge (1966), on King Road West, off McKenzie River Drive
- Pengra Bridge (1936), near Jasper, off Jasper-Lowell Road on Place Road
- Unity Bridge (1936), further on Jasper-Lowell Road beyond Pengra

- Lowell Bridge (1945), adjacent to Jasper-Lowell Road near Highway 58
- Parvin Bridge (1921), on Parvin Road in the same general area as Pengra, Unity, and Lowell
- Currin Bridge (1920), crossing Row River at the intersection of Row River Road and Layng Road (some sources call it Lang Road), east of Cottage Grove. It replaced a bridge first built here in 1883.
- Mosby Creek (1920), on Layng Road not far from Currin, near Mosby Creek Road. This is Lane County's oldest bridge and one of the few supported by wooden pilings instead of concrete abutments.
- Stewart Bridge (1930), on Mosby Creek Road at the intersection with Garoutte Road, 3½ miles from Cottage Grove.
- Dorena Bridge (1949), off Government Road. Built to span the Row River at the upper end of Dorena Dam Reservoir, it was bypassed in 1974 by a concrete bridge.
- Coyote Creek Bridge (1922), southwest of Eugene on Battle Creek Road
- Wildcat Bridge (1925), off Highway 126 east of Florence, over Siuslaw Road to Austa Road.
- Office Bridge, north of Oakridge on North Fork Road. Privately owned by a local timber company, it is the largest covered bridge in the county.
- Chambers Bridge, privately owned, south of Cottage Grove near Highway 99. It is the last covered railroad bridge in Oregon, but now is sitting neglected and is a target of vandalism on an abandoned right-of-way owned by Oregon Electric Railway.

Wineries

A little bit of France—
in Oregon

The drink which was considered sophisticated in Portland during the 1950s was bourbon, a sour mash bourbon, a bitter elixir in my opinion. The more you were able to drink, the more of a man you were supposed to be. And if you could down a shot of bourbon or blended whiskey with a beer chaser, you were a "real man." Bourbon and other whiskeys were linked with manliness. If you drank anything less potent, or considered to be less potent, such as gin, you would be marked "a sissy." Intolerance in those days was considered to be a virtuous attribute.

You can now imagine what you were thought of if you drank wine, an even less potent beverage. So the drink in the '50s was whiskey, straight, glass filled to the brim—a holdover from the Old West. Beer was available but only in three or four brands, and any resemblance to East Coast beer was pure accident. Imported beer was unavailable.

Coors, brewed in Colorado, at that time was not sold in Oregon. Hence it was considered the luxury beer, and when you traveled to California where it was sold you made sure you brought back a double six-pack or more. The local brands were Lucky Lager, Blitz, Olympia, Heidelberg, Hamms, and a few others. Budweiser and Miller were still trying to get a foothold here.

The favorite whiskeys among the locals were such blends as Three Feathers, Seagrams, Early Times, and Jim Beam. The private downtown Portland social clubs stocked Jack Daniels, a sour mash, and other high-priced bourbons for their member clientele. The clubs referred to Jack Daniels in almost reverent tones, and as one who could not even stomach the smell of bourbon I wondered what lay ahead for this young reporter from the East Coast.

When I first became enamored of journalism, I was given a friendly warning by none other than my mother. Even though she was protected from the evils of the outside world, she graded journalists at one level above evil incarnate because of their reputation as excessive drinkers. Now, my parents didn't consider alcohol evil because we did have wine at dinner. Even when we were children they permitted us to taste and drink an ounce or so on occasion. But they objected to the overindulgence, the drinking before, during, and after meals, the abuse. On occasion my father would serve scotch to guests, but that was rare, for most of our friends and relatives preferred wine and drank it, in moderation, only with their evening or noonday meals.

Now, what does all this have to do with wine and with the Oregon wine country?

First of all, Oregon in the '50s was not thinking of itself as a wine-growing country. The main reason was that many were of the opinion that the rain prevented the growth of wine grapes, even though we were growing Concord grapes and producing berry wines during that period, and still are.

Another reason was that Oregonians of that period didn't consider themselves wine drinkers. Those who were known to drink wine were either ethnics (in those days called foreigners) or the homeless (then called either hoboes or winos). The latter term created a prolonged prejudice against wine. After all, no one wanted to be compared with people who slept it off in some doorway or alley, often still clutching a bottle of wine. The police called these people "winos," and it was daily routine to pick them up and cart them off to the city jail at SW Second and Oak in Portland, where they were generally given 30 days in jail. During that time they worked off their sentences performing menial labor, either for the city or some political crony of the establishment.

Thus the term *wino* was born, an egregious stereotype. Whole neighborhoods lived out their lives without ever admitting to knowing anything about wine, much less drinking it.

So for many years after I arrived in Portland in the mid-'50s, wine was seldom seen at dinner tables of Portland homes or, for that matter, sold in the better grocery outlets. They did have it in some of the Italian-American homes. Many Portlanders who knew Italians and wanted to show their affection for Italian-Americans would say they drank wine with their "Eye-talian" friends. They called the wine "Dago red."

In today's ethnic-conscious world, the word *Dago* would be considered an ethnic slur and rightly so. It is seldom heard or used today.

Much of the credit for popularizing wine in Oregon and making it reputable goes not only to the gradual influx of wine growers into the Willamette Valley and other western Oregon farmlands but to the new breed of wine distributors, who made their money selling the widely advertised California brands.

These distributors quietly began importing premium wines from France and Italy. The palates of Portlanders were being educated. Soon the rest of the state followed. Al C. Giusti, whose father founded the Italian Importing Company on SE Grand Avenue near Belmont in Portland, was to become the city's leading wine entrepreneur and a notable civic booster.

I remember how a former colleague once wrote in his column that only "winos and Italians" drank wine. I personally called the columnist and demanded an apology. I got him to meet with Al Giusti. This initial meeting subsequently led to a long friendship between the two. Wine had gotten a new convert and received better press from then on.

As the '50s faded quietly from the scene, a new breed began to make itself seen and heard, and with it a new lifestyle that was to change behavior for years to come. The '60s, the age of the hippie, dawned brightly with the shattering of many past traditions and intolerances. Wine started to become the beverage of the young. With it, new appetites were being fashioned, and soon what had once been identified with certain ethnics became "de rigeur."

Although most Oregonians at that time still were ignoring wines and didn't consider them worthy of their palates, many came to appreciate fine wines through their travels in Europe. They more they traveled, the more they realized that a complete meal must include wine. To Europeans it would be uncouth to omit it.

Slowly but surely, wine was becoming popular.

The California winemakers were in the forefront and reaping the cash harvest. Competition and population growth were forcing many of the small California vintners to look for less expensive real estate on which to grow their grapes.

Some looked north, and those with courage and know-how made the trip. In the '60s, searching for new grape land in the Northwest was a pioneering adventure that could spell disaster or riches.

A young man from California, Richard Sommers, was one of the first modern grape wine growers in the state. He is believed to have been the actual first, coming in the late '50s and planting the first white Riesling and Pinot vines in the red foothill soil of Roseburg in 1960. He crushed his first grapes

in 1962 and then added such varieties as Cabernet Sauvignon, Pinot Chardonnay, Sauvignon Blanc, Pinot Blanc, Zinfandel, and Gewürztraminer.

Sommers maintained that the famous old world wines were produced in a climate much like the Roseburg area, where melting snow and adequate rainfall made irrigation unnecessary. His Hillcrest Winery was not far from the site of the Adolph Doerner Winery, which operated from 1890 to 1952.

Sommers concentrated on varietal wines, while Doerner made a blended wine. Shortly before his death, Doerner confided to Sommers, "There's no trouble growing grapes in this country, the big problem is in selling them."

With the coming of the Hillcrest Winery, and building on the early efforts of Doerner, Oregon began to attract young vintners not only to the Roseburg area but farther north, to the fertile valleys of Yamhill County and the surrounding countryside.

One young vintner who eventually became widely respected and even revered for his talents began planting premium wine grapes at McMinnville. At age 26, David Lett, with his wife Diana, established the Eyrie Vineyards in 1966. "Next to my wife," he was quoted as saying in an article in *The Oregonian*, "my first love is pinot noir."

It was dedicated vintners like Lett who became the new breed of farmer in a valley that had made its reputation in years past as one of the world's leading producers of filberts or hazelnuts. (Dundee was the filbert capital.) Eventually it was to become a premium producing region of some of the world's leading pinot noir.

When I was a reporter, a farm writer to be more exact, during the violence and turmoil of the '60s, I would, on occasion, write about more tranquil subjects. Writing about some of Oregon's pioneer winemakers—and there were only a few then—was a change that I enjoyed. Although at the time the interest about wine in Oregon was minimal, the articles did stimulate some response from both doubters and dreamers. My interviews convinced me that Oregon wines had a future.

When I visited France in 1987 and made a brief stop in the celebrated wine country of the Burgoyne Valley, I was especially struck by its similarity to Oregon. I first felt this kinship in the historic and much publicized city of Dijon—not so much with the town itself but with the surrounding countryside, which was laced with rows and rows of fruit-bearing vines. The day remains vivid in my memory. It was overcast. A mist concealed the hillside, with its summer fruit hanging in lush abundance on very old vines. From these vines came the juice which brought acclaim from the connoisseurs of the world.

Little did I realize that soon I was to be vindicated in my frequent boast that Oregon would one day be not only the land of Tillamook Cheese and ocean breeze but of wine as well.

"Now, the pinot of Oregon . . . that is a wine. I know of your wine." The comment came from an unsolicited and highly expert source.

Jean-Pierre Renard, a conseiller oenophile of Dijon, had been elaborating on the highly regarded wines of the Burgoyne Valley. When he heard I was from Oregon, his eyes took on a warmer glow, and he smiled at me, a very genuine smile. I then heard the name of my state pronounced beautifully in that enviable French accent.

"Orāgōn! I know it well. You have exemplary wines, mon ami." His voice had the ring of sincerity.

"Only a few months ago, one of your wine growers was here," he continued. "You are going to have a great pinot noir with that '83 vintage." He wanted to share that revelation with me.

I had hardly expected to hear raves about Oregon wines from one whose life was selling the wines of the Burgoyne Valley. I had been impatient to get on with the remainder of my trip, but instead had been delayed, pleasantly as it turned out, by someone who wanted me to know that I lived in a region of the world that had become a new wine-producing phenomenon.

Prior to that time, I had had little success in convincing anyone that Oregon wines should be respected and admired. This compliment from a vintner of Renard's stature was for me a personal triumph. I felt instantly vindicated for my years of fruitlessly extolling the potential of Oregon wines.

Today, Oregonians consume about 8 million gallons of wine annually and produce more than 800,000 gallons. This is more than triple the gallonage of the early 1980s.

Following are the Oregon wineries and their locations.

Information is current as of press date. You are advised to call for most current information.

Adams Vineyard Winery, 1922 NW Pettygrove Street, Portland, OR 97209, (503) 294-0606.

No, they don't grow grapes on Pettygrove Street. Carol and Peter Adams grow near Newberg. No tasting room at this small winery, but visitors are welcome by appointment.

Adelsheim Vineyard, 22150 NE Quarter Mile Lane, Newberg, OR 97132, (503) 538-3652.

No tasting room, but two annual events, usually in June and November. Write for invitation in advance.

Airlie Winery, 15305 Dunn Forest Road, Monmouth, OR 97361, (503) 838-6013.

Tasting room, group tours, open weekdays by appointment, open weekends except January and February. Call or write for festival information.

Alpine Vineyards, 25904 Green Peak Road, Alpine, OR 97456, (503) 424-5851.

Near Corvallis. Winery open daily except closed Christmas through January, tasting room also on the Newport bayfront.

Amity Vineyards, 18150 Amity Vineyards Road SE, Amity, OR 97101-9603, (503) 835-2362.

Open June-October daily, November-May weekends, closed Christmas through January. Tasting also at Lawrence Gallery near McMinnville.

Arterberry Winery, 905 E. 10th Ave., PO Box 772, McMinnville, OR 97128, (503) 472-1587 or 244-0695.

Tasting room. Open weekends April-December, closed January-March.

Ashland Vineyards, 2775 East Main Street, Ashland, OR 97520, (503) 488-0088.

Tasting room near Shakespearean theaters. Open Wednesday-Sunday April-October, weekends November-December and February-March, closed January.

Autumn Wind Vineyard, 15225 North Valley Road, PO Box 666, Newberg, OR 97132, (503) 538-6931.

Open weekends, open weekdays by group appointment, closed mid-December through February.

Bethel Heights Vineyard, 6060 Bethel Heights Road NW, Salem, OR 97304, (503) 581-2262.

Open Tuesday-Sunday March-December; closed Mondays, Thanksgiving, Christmas, January-February.

Bridgeview Vineyards, 4210 Holland Loop Rd., Cave Junction, OR 97523, (503) 592-4688 or 592-4698.

Visitors to winery by appointment only, tasting room on Highway 199 in Kerby.

Broadley Vineyards, 265 South 5th (Highway 99), Monroe, OR 97456, (503) 847-5934.

Open Tuesday-Sunday, closed January and Mondays.

Callahan Ridge Winery, 340 Busenbark Lane, Roseburg, OR 97470, (503) 673-7901.

Open daily April-October, closed November-March.

Chateau Benoit Winery, N.E. Mineral Springs Road, Carlton, OR 97111, (503) 864-2991 or 864-3666.

Open daily, year-round. Phone appointments requested for groups of 15 or more.

Cooper Mountain Vineyard, Rt. 3, Box 1036 (Grabhorn Road), Beaverton, OR 97007, (503) 649-0027.

Visitors welcome, but by appointment only.

Elk Cove Vineyards, 27751 NW Olson Rd., Gaston, OR 97119, (503) 985-7760.

Open daily year-round except closed Thanksgiving, Christmas, New Year's Day. Also tasting rooms at Dundee and Hood River.

Ellendale Winery, 99W at Rickreall Road, Rickreall, OR 97371, (503) 623-6835.

Open daily except Thanksgiving, Christmas and New Year's Day, tours also by appointment at Dallas, OR.

Eola Hills Wine Cellars, 501 South Pacific Highway West, Rickreall, OR 97371, (503) 623-2405.

Open daily May-late November, closed late November-April.

Evesham Wood Vineyard, 2995 Michigan City Ave., West Salem, OR 97304, (503) 371-8478.

Annual events in May and November, otherwise visits by appointment only.

The Eyrie Vineyards, 935 East 10th St., McMinnville, OR 97128, (503) 472-6315 or 864-2410.

Pioneering Oregon vineyard since 1966, annual event late November, otherwise visits by appointment.

Forgeron Vineyard, 89697 Sheffler Road, Elmira, OR 97437, (503) 935-1117 or 935-3530.

Open daily June-September, weekends October-December and February-May, closed January.

Foris Vineyard, 654 Kendall Road, Cave Junction, OR 97523, (503) 592-3752.

Open daily year-round except closed some major holidays, call ahead.

Girardet Wine Cellars, 895 Reston Road, Roseburg, OR 97470, (503) 679-7252.

Open daily May-September, Saturday only October-April, closed late December through January.

Glen Creek Winery, 6057 Orchard Heights Road NW, Salem, OR 97304, (503) 371-9463.

Open year-round Tuesday through Sunday except closed Thanksgiving, Christmas, New Year's Day, Easter.

Henry Estate Winery, 687 Hubbard Creek Road, Highway 9, PO Box 26, Umpqua, OR 97486, (503) 459-5120 or 459-3614.

Open daily year-round except closed major holidays.

Hidden Springs Winery, 9360 SE Eola Hills Road, Amity, OR 97101, (503) 835-2782.

Open weekends only March-November, closed December-February. Also outlets in Albany and Valley Junction.

Hillcrest Vineyard, 240 Vineyard Lane, Roseburg, OR 97470, (503) 673-3709.

Open year-round except closed major holidays, call ahead.

Hinman Vineyards, 27012 Briggs Hills Road, Eugene, OR 97405, (503) 345-1945.

Open daily except closed Christmas to New Year's Day. Facilities for weddings and private parties may be rented.

Honeywood Winery, 501 14th St. SE, Salem, OR 97301, (503)362-4111.

Established 1934, oldest producing winery in Oregon. Also tasting room at Lincoln City, both open daily.

Hood River Vineyards, 4693 Westwood Drive, Hood River, OR 97031, (503) 386-3772 or 386-3949.

Open daily March-December, closed January-February.

Knudsen Erath, 17000 NE Knudsen Lane, Dundee, OR 97115, (503) 538-3318.

One of America's largest producers of Pinot Noir. Open daily except Thanksgiving, Christmas, New Year's Day and "when the well freezes."

Lange Winery, 18380 NE Buena Vista, Dundee, OR 97115, (503) 538-6476.

Visitors welcome, but by appointment only.

Laurel Ridge Winery, Rt 1, Box 255, David Hill Road, Forest Grove, OR 97116, (503) 359-5436.

Open Tuesday-Sunday May-October, weekends November-April, closed January.

Marquam Hill Vineyards Winery, 35803 S Highway 213, Molalla, OR 97038, (503) 829-6677.

Open late May through Labor Day daily, weekends September-December and February-May, closed January.

Meridian, 2920 NW Scenic Drive, Albany, OR 97321, (503) 928-1009.

Visitors welcome by appointment.

Montinore Vineyards, Route 3, Box 193W (Dilley Road), Forest Grove, OR 97116, (503) 359-5012.

Visitors welcome by appointment.

Oak Knoll Winery, Route 6, Box 184, Hillsboro, OR 97123, (503) 648-8198.

Open Wednesday through Sunday, Monday and Tuesday by appointment. Also outlet at Lincoln City.

Panther Creek Cellars, 1501 E 14th St., McMinnville, OR 97128, (503) 472-8080.

Visitors welcome by appointment only.

Ponzi Vineyards, Vandermost Road, Route 1, Box 842, Beaverton, OR 97007, (503) 628-1227.

Many special events, winery open weekends, sales office weekdays, closed January and holidays.

Rex Hill Vineyards, Inc., 30835 N Highway 99W, Newberg, OR 97132, (503) 538-0666.

Open April-December daily, February-March Friday-Sunday, closed January.

St. Innocent Winery, 2701 22d St. SE, Salem, OR 97302, (503) 378-1526.

Open weekends May-December, closed January-April.

Schwarzenberg Vineyards, 11975 Smithfield Road, Dallas, OR 97338, (503) 623-6420.

Open May-October Tuesday-Sunday, weekends November-December and February-April, closed January except by appointment.

Serendipity Cellars Winery, 15275 Forest Road, Monmouth, OR 97361, (503) 838-4284.

Open May-November Wednesday through Monday, December-April weekends, closed Tuesdays.

Shafer Vineyard Cellars, Star Route Box 269, Forest Grove, OR 97116, (503) 357-6604.

Open June-September daily, October-May weekends only.

Siskiyou Vineyards, 6220 Caves Highway, Cave Junction, OR 97523, (503) 592-3727.

Open daily except Easter, Thanksgiving, Christmas, New Year's Day. Additional outlet in Ashland.

Sokol Blosser Winery, 5000 Sokol Blosser Lane, Dundee, OR 97115, (503) 864-2282.

Open year-round. Tours hourly.

Tualatin Vineyards, Route 1, Box 339 (Seavey Road), Forest Grove, OR 97116, (503) 357-5005.

Open daily except closed January and holidays.

Tyee Wine Cellars, 26335 Greenberry Road, Corvallis, OR 97333, (503) 753-8754.

Open weekends May-October, closed November-April except by appointment.

Veritas Vineyard, 31190 NE Veritas Lane, Newberg, OR 97132, (503) 538-1470.

Open daily June-August, all other times by appointment.

Weisinger's, 3150 Siskiyou, Ashland, OR 97520, (503) 488-5989.

Open year-round Tuesday-Sunday, closed Monday.

Yamhill Valley Vineyards, 16250 Oldsville Road, off Highway 18, McMinnville, OR 97128, (503) 843-3100.

May-Thanksgiving Tuesday-Sunday, March-April weekends, closed December-February and Mondays.

Central Oregon

The "everything" vacation land

This part of the state is known as "the Other Oregon," where there are giant lava flows, miles and miles of high desert, alpine lakes, and snow-capped peaks, where the summers are warm and the winters dry and cold.

To me, there is one person who epitomizes Central Oregon.

I had just gotten off a chartered tour bus with a Portland delegation of agribusiness people. We were in the middle of a high plateau, some 4,000 feet above sea level, staring at a prehistoric geological wonder called Fort Rock. There was a town nearby with that name, but it was not in view.

A tall, broad-shouldered man with a friendly grin and a twinkle in his eye greeted us. He wore a broad-brimmed rancher's hat, boots, a blue checkered shirt, western style, and Levis.

"Hi, name's Reub Long. Welcome to Fort Rock." His extended grip displayed hands that were rough, big, but friendly.

He told us how much he enjoyed living in Fort Rock. He had been there all his life and hoped to remain there. He was growing alfalfa.

"Don't you ever have a desire to travel?" I asked, knowing that staying here overnight would be more solitude than I needed.

"Why? When I'm already here?"

Back then Reub Long had not yet become famous for the books that he wrote on the Oregon desert with E. R. Jackman. Today, one of the main exhibit halls at the Oregon state fairgrounds is named the E. R. Jackman–Reub Long building.

These two men were here when the landmark in the Bend country was the Pilot Butte Inn in downtown Bend. The tourist draw then was Paulina Lake near La Pine, named after the famous Indian chief Pah-ni-neh, who was murdered in cold blood by renegade white men during the early settler days.

Mount Bachelor was just coming into favor as a skiing center, and the resort complexes of Black Butte and Sunriver were still in the planning stages. It was a land for the angler and camper and hunter. Skiers and city folks were just beginning to discover it.

The Californians came later with their tail-fin Cadillacs, declaring they wanted to become "Oregonized," anxious to leave behind a land that had given them wealth but apparently not the quality of life they had hoped to enjoy in their remaining years.

The Central Oregonians were somewhat prepared for the rush of Californians because there were a few greenhorns like me from the East Coast who had earlier discovered this land of plenty. We were the appetizers to a bittersweet meal that was yet to come. But many Central Oregonians were very hospitable and took pains to make me familiar with an alien world. One was my friend, Jack Steiwer, who still lives in a small town called Fossil, not too far from another town called Spray, which is located not too far from Condon, in a beautiful display of rolling and rugged mountains. Steiwer is a tall, very tall, Gary Cooper-like man who in his youthful days could negotiate a kayak with precise skill through some of the most daring rapids on the John Day River while still enjoying the after-flavor of some good old western bourbon.

Over the years I got to visit Jack at his home in Fossil. He lived in one of the biggest houses in Fossil. Had this house been in the Portland West Hills, a well-to-do neighborhood, it would easily be the historic landmark of the block. Here it was in the center of town, framed by towering trees that offered a refreshing change to the brown-pink hills rolling and dipping around us in this area known as the Clarno Valley. For miles I saw a vast spread of land reaching out to the great ranges of mountains uplifted far away against a clear Central Oregon sky. Not too far from Jack's house on a small hill is the Fossil school, and behind the school building was a heaping pile of fossils, the ancient treasure for which this town was named. I remember helping myself to some of these precious rocks. In these more enlightened times this practice has probably been prohibited.

I will always remember the town of Fossil, and I am sure some of the residents of that town will never forget me—the big-city hick who came to Fossil in search of adventure on the rapids of the John Day River. Everything went well on that rafting trip except on the last day, when I got back to town and discovered that my old Volkswagen fastback refused to function. I had had trouble with it before and had always been able to get it to kick over. Now I

was in Fossil and no mechanic would touch it. My patience dried up, I decided to leave it there and buy a new car...in Fossil! The fact that I decided to abandon my clunker and buy a new car from one of the town's two dealers was a news event. My photo was taken and a story written about me in the local newspaper. Indeed, according to Jack, the transaction is one of the town's great stories. I am remembered not for my courage in shooting the rapids or my feature stories on the beauty of the Clarno Valley but for my impulsive purchase of a new car from a dealer who also ran a mechanic shop and had an inventory of only three cars.

When I am in Central Oregon or even Eastern Oregon I feel I am in the presence of a way of life that has not changed much since the first days I rolled into this state in my 1954 Ford coupe. Within a few years I was writing about subjects that I never knew existed.

I remember my first meeting of the Oregon Cattlemen's Association, which took place in Redmond about 10 miles from Bend, the skiing capital of Central Oregon. There I learned that cattlemen work hard, play tough, eat hearty, and don't wear ties. This last fact I learned the hard way. When I showed up at the drinking hole wearing a blue blazer, a button-down shirt, and a tie, things began to happen. After I was greeted warmly and handed a drink, which I think was bourbon, a rancher by the name of Davis placed his long arm around my shoulder, and smiled. No sooner had I returned the smile than I saw a huge scissors appear from nowhere, snip my tie below the knot, and disappear. Davis laughingly told me, "Out here, in God's country, we don't wear ties. Welcome."

I don't know whether I ever put the decapitated tie on my expense account or not. However, from that day of initiation I had easy access into the inner sanctums of the Oregon Cattlemen's Association. Little did they know that I was ignorant not only of the dress code but also of most ranching terms. I did learn fast, and soon became one of the more respected writers of agriculture in the Northwest.

Traveling in this part of the state was always an exhilarating experience. This is because Central Oregon has many things going for it, most of them relating to sunshine. Summers are hot and dry, but it turns cold at night. In the winter, dry, deep snow blesses the mountains. Most spots on this high desert country count 200 to 300 days of sunshine annually and only about 12 inches of rain. Millions of years ago, this was a semitropical rain forest, but today, it is a semiarid steppe.

Most often, when Portlanders get that hankering for warm sun, they think of Kah-Nee-Ta, the resort made popular by the Warm Springs Indian Tribe. When the resort was developed about 25 years ago it was not considered a "sure thing." The reason: most people—I would say about 99 percent of the non-Indian population—would not consider vacationing on an Indian reservation.

The idea for the resort was the brainchild of the Warm Springs tribe, and more specifically one of its members, Vern Jackson, whom I knew on a casual basis.

I had never been to an Indian reservation and I hadn't seen any Indians before I arrived in Oregon back in the mid-'50s. One day, the same tour bus which took me to see Reub Long at Fort Rock also stopped at Warm Springs. We didn't travel into the heart of the Indian land but remained on the highway and just ventured out of the bus a few feet to do some rubbernecking. The rising heat began to irk me, but the anticipation of meeting a member of the tribe—a real Indian—eliminated any annoying discomfort I might have experienced.

Vern Jackson was about five feet and a few inches, heavily tanned, broad shouldered and paunchy. He began to tell stories of the tribe and the vision of new economic times ahead. The tribe was experiencing some growth, but Jackson realized that the growth was only the beginning of what could come from the land.

"Some day we will have a resort here, and many will come from many places because Warm Springs is the land of the eternal sun," he said. At the time, none of us really believed him. I simply took notes and more notes, and when I returned to Portland wrote a story about the resort that supposedly would be built one day on the Indian reservation of the Confederated Tribes of Warm Springs. I think my editor felt I had too much sun and was glad to see me back on our side of the mountain, in the land of eternal rain.

Vern Jackson was right, but unfortunately he never lived to see how successful the resort turned out to be. Today, because of the resort and other ventures, the tribe is one of the more successful in the Northwest. In 1993 it opened with much fanfare the Northwest's finest museum of Indian artifacts.

The Kah-Nee-Ta resort is about 120 miles from Portland off Highway 26, a bit far away for a one-day excursion. Yet many Portlanders do it in a single day, and gladly, when they feel their bones softening in the winter rains.

For those who can stay longer than a day, there are tepees, cabins, and a posh lodge with its own pool. Indians in traditional regalia make frequent appearances to drum, dance, and conduct salmon bakes. There is golf, hiking, and horseback riding. Let me warn you, however, about the tepees. At first, it would seem like a jolly evening to spend camping in a tepee. I tried it. I wasn't alone. I wanted my wife and two small children to share in the experience and have something they would remember for some time to come. I think to this day they do remember that night when I started a campfire inside the tepee so we could fully experience the total package. Was I wrong? The place filled with smoke despite the air vent at the top. We were living—all four of us—in an area the size of a small bedroom. It was not a dream vacation. There was no kitchen and no bathroom inside the tepee. The only thing we had was space and not much of it. I think we spent only one night there and opted the next day for a cozy room with running water and all the other amenities.

However, I look back and consider myself a survivor of those early outings. The one thing I can say for them is that closeness with the outdoors made me more passionate about the attraction of the indoors. I know this is anathema to the tradition which exists here in the wonderful Northwest, but I still enjoy being awakened every morning with the sight of the city before me.

Nevertheless, I consider Central Oregon to be the ideal outdoor recreation area, with everything except ocean beaches, all available in great variety.

A unique experience, at least for me, lies northwest of Bend, on Highway 20. Here, you're entering the Deschutes National Forest, where you encounter the little town of Sisters. What are those funny animals you see in this area? They are llamas. Central Oregon claims to be the llama capital of America, and the biggest of all llama ranches is at Sisters. At one time, Kim Novak, a popular film actress of the '50s and '60s, had a llama ranch in Central Oregon, and perhaps she still does. To the folk of Central Oregon, she wouldn't be a celebrity, just another rancher.

A turnoff from Highway 20 takes you to Black Butte, a favorite resort. Yet a further turnoff leads to picturesque Camp Sherman on the Metolius River, which flows out of a bubbling spring on the north face of the volcanic cinder cone of Black Butte. The upper reaches of the Metolius possess a quality more remarkable than its constant above-40-degree temperature. It is the most tranquilizing river in the entire state, and anglers from all over the Northwest go there for its renowned therapeutic qualities. The fishing is also legendary.

Every river has a personality, at least in Oregon. The Rogue in southern Oregon roars. The Miami on the coast meanders. The Columbia rolls on—at least, Woody Guthrie said it does, in a song he wrote back in the 1930s.

The Metolius soothes. It is not very wide and only moderately deep. It is a cheerful, contented river, burbling along quietly, devoid of fuss or furor. My first introduction to the Metolius was when I was a new arrival in Oregon and my neighbor, a retired U.S. Army general and prominent Portland attorney, Lamar Tooze, invited me and my family to spend a weekend in his home on the Metolius.

I remember taking a photograph of General Tooze—"Gompie" as my kids used to call him—as he was strolling across one of the bridges spanning the river. The contentment, the pleasure, the freedom, and the relaxation all expressed on his face as he walked across that bridge came through vividly in the photograph. He was so proud of that photograph that he decided to hang it on his office wall where others could share in that moment of pure joy.

We had a fine time that weekend, and the memory of the woods, the river, and the crackling fire in the Tooze home will always remain with me.

One of the great attractions in Central Oregon that has only been around since the late 1960s is the High Desert Museum. The museum, located near Bend, combines indoor and outdoor exhibits on 150 acres amid the Deschutes Forest. The indoor section is dominated by the Earl A. Chiles Center on the Spirit of the West. Here, visitors "walk through time" to recall various stages in the opening of the American West through lifesized re-creations of scenes from the past. These follow the passage of the sun, from early morning in a Paiute Indian camp to sunset on an 1880 cattle ranch. Titles include Native People, Fur Trade, Overland Migration, Exploration and Survey, Mining, Settlement, and Buckaroo.

The outdoor section features 20 acres of nature trails with live animals and birds, along with authentic artifacts of the westward migration. The museum is an interactive one, not a passive display, scheduling ongoing programs, lectures, and interpretive features.

From the standpoint of sheer concentration of geologic marvels, the Newberry National Volcanic Monument is the place to see. It was made a national monument only recently, in November 1990, and is managed by the Deschutes National Forest.

In some ways the monument defines Central Oregon. It is vast, more than 50,000 acres dominated by the 500 square miles of the Newberry Volcano. Now extinct, the volcano erupted thousands of times over the past half-million years, well into the era when Indians populated the land.

The Inn of the Seventh Mountain resort lies near the monument's northern boundary. The Deschutes River forms its northwestern boundary. The easiest access for visitors is from Highway 97, which cuts through the middle of the Monument about 11 miles south of Bend.

Just off Highway 97 is the Lava Lands Visitor Center, a concentrated experience of interpretive trails and displays. More than 95 percent of the world's volcanic features are present here, including, beneath the ground, the rumblings of geothermal activity. Some 6,000 years ago hot molten lava coursed from the northwest corner of the volcano, overwhelming a forest. The result is a field of "lava casts" or molds of these ancient trees.

Within the crater of the volcano is Paulina Lake and its sister, East Lake. Also within the crater is a giant flow of obsidian, the black glass-like material that the Indians flaked off for arrowheads and cutting tools.

A lifetime could be spent sampling all the attractions of Central Oregon. There is world-class rock climbing at Smith Rock, horizon scanning from Paulina Peak, spelunking in the numerous lava tube caves, whitewater rafting on the Deschutes. The potentialities run alphabetically from backpacking to windsurfing. Sixteen golf courses lie within easy driving range.

If people from the population centers of the Willamette Valley could reach this high desert country as quickly and easily as they can reach the coast, sun-washed Central Oregon might well outstrip the beach as the state's most popular recreational destination. Those who take the little extra time and effort required insist that Central Oregon is vacation heaven.

Rodeo

*Profitable bull market—
if you don't lose your
balance*

Pendleton, like Calgary and Cheyenne, haunts the fancy of the imaginative rodeo goer more than all the other rodeo centers of the West. The prospect of seeing a rodeo in Pendleton made my heart beat.

Pendleton was a legend in Oregon rodeo history. I was to realize and share the dream of many. There is no greater splendor in Oregon, or the Pacific Northwest for that matter, than September in the Blue Mountains and rodeo in the air at Pendleton.

The only hesitancy I had about attending a rodeo was my complete and unequivocal ignorance of the sport. However, I soon learned I didn't need to know how many minutes or seconds a Jim Shoulders or any other bronc buster was required to remain aloft to be a winner. Just the fact that men were pitted against rearing horses and ferocious bulls in death-defying contest was all I needed to know.

It was the '60s, and the fiesta mood of rodeo was everywhere. I considered myself fortunate to find such a rare bit of entertainment, set against the stubble of golden wheat fields, the music of high school bands, and the clip-clopping of horses' hooves on asphalt streets. Thousands come from all over Oregon and beyond to take in the excitement of the famous Pendleton Round-Up and the Happy Canyon Pageant staged by the Confederated Tribes of Umatilla.

I saw bulldogging, saddle bronc riding, calf roping, and steer roping, and when it was over I was no longer a tenderfoot.

The one thing that impressed me the most was the toughness of the cowboys, who were able to endure physical punishment from an animal that was easily 10 to 20 times stronger and heavier. It was a David and Goliath match, and most of the time Goliath won.

Some of the cowboys were not at all towering figures when they were off a horse. But I had the utmost respect for the physical capabilities of these men who roped and tossed four-legged critters to the ground for a living.

One evening, after filing several lengthy stories to my paper, I decided to scan the nearby "watering holes" in the search for relaxation and recreation.

The old Temple Hotel was still the big favorite and one of the livelier places this side of the Columbia River.

I had no sooner walked in than a comely young woman with an obvious plan cuddled up to me and announced it was time for the two of us to dance. In those days, the men did the asking. Her invitation took me by surprise, but I obliged, for a refusal would have been an error in social graces.

As we were negotiating a fast two-step, the music suddenly changed its beat to something soothing and slow. In those days, dancing was cheek to cheek and being the slightest distance apart was an affront to your partner. As the music played on I forgot about my work, my deadlines, my obligations. She was a marvelous dancer. My esteem for eastern Oregon women, at this moment, was limitless. The music played on.

Without warning the smooth serenade was shattered by what I thought was galloping hooves across the dance floor. It was a horse, I thought. It must have been let loose as a prank. The cowboys were notorious pranksters. But it was not a horse. Something more lethal was advancing toward the center of the floor where I was closely embracing my new-found partner. "Oh my God," she said. "It's my boyfriend."

I didn't want an introduction because it was quite obvious the boyfriend was not in a social frame of mind. When the word "boyfriend" was uttered I parted without the usual goodbyes. I darted for the exit and kept on going. I do remember returning to my room unscathed but not unbowed. The next morning I steadied my nerves with the traditional cowboy breakfast of hot biscuits, home fries, bacon, and scrambled eggs, amidst the security of other festival goers. It was a typical eastern Oregon morning in September, clear and sunlit. It was great to be alive to bear witness to another day.

On this day, under a bright September sun, an estimated 6,000 persons turned out to welcome wild and whooping cowboys and scores of the wickedest horses in the Northwest. It was the golden anniversary of the Pendleton Round-Up, and I knew that cowboys were going to be pretty well occupied for the next day or so with bronc busting, calf roping, and whatever else keeps them lean, sinewy, and mean, if provoked.

The action went fast in the opening go-round of competition. Later in the evening the fans were entertained by the Happy Canyon Show put on by members of the Umatilla Confederated tribes.

When the first "Whoopie" sounded in the crowded stadium, the greatest cowboy show on earth came to life with all the color and pageantry that had made it famous since it had first opened its gates in 1910.

Then there was the Westward Ho Parade. Every color known was sparkling as Pendleton put on its best parade dress. There was music for the old timers and music for the young set. Ragtime and bop filled the air, played by smartly dressed high school bands. There was a surrey with a fringe on top, and there was one without. There was a prairie schooner and a four-wheeled phaeton for the pioneer men and women. There were cowgirls, cowpokes, rodeo queens, and plenty of fun, laughter, and whoop-de-do.

It was the early '60s, and the Round-Up was doing its part to bring entertainment to the folks of the Blue Mountain country and to the thousands who from elsewhere came to join in the celebration.

Today, Oregon and neighboring Washington field some of the finest cowboy rodeo talent to be found anywhere. There are more than 250 active contestants competing in more than 40 CRPC rodeos in Oregon, Washington, and Idaho. They all are part of the Columbia River Prorodeo Circuit, one of 12 circuits of the Professional Rodeo Cowboy Association.

Following is a list of the cities where CRPC rodeos are regularly presented, along with the usual months. For information, you can call those great people at the Pendleton Round-Up office at (503) 276-2553 or 1-800-45 RODEO. The address is 1205 SW Court, PO Box 609, Pendleton, OR 97801.

Also, there are other rodeos throughout the region, some sanctioned by smaller sanctioning bodies, some just collected together with no particular sanctioning. The "usual" CRPC schedule follows:

January: Portland. February: Kennewick, Washington. April: Prineville, Oregon. May: Coulee City, Washington. June: Tonasket, Colville, and Newport in Washington; Union, Sisters, and Roseburg in Oregon. July: Molalla, St. Paul, Elgin, Prineville, The Dalles, Joseph, and Hillsboro in Oregon; Toppenish, Cheney, and Longview in Washington. August: Canby, Hermiston, and Heppner in Oregon; Tacoma, Omak, Moses Lake, Bremerton, and Kennewick in Washington; Coeur d'Alene, Idaho. September: Pendleton Round-Up; Walla Walla, Ellensburg, Spokane, Othello, Puyallup, and Yakima in Washington; Lewiston, Idaho. October: Central Point, Oregon.

Crater Lake

Deeper than deep, bluer than blue, relic of a turbulent past

When I came to Oregon in the early 1950s, I was at first indifferent to the beauty that was pointed out to me by those who lived here. I had innate tastes and was fond of artistic forms. However, I lacked an appreciation for open spaces and majestic rock formations and deep blue mountain lakes.

Crater Lake was to me a place high in altitude and low in temperature—frightfully cold. My in-laws had taken me to this lake, wanting me to appreciate this ancient volcano, and even though I never had seen the remnants of any volcano before, I was not impressed. I could not experience awe in the face of what was simply to me a deep mountain lake high in the middle of an ancient volcano.

But I was bored only because I was not giving this scene my close personal consideration, not giving it an opportunity to excite my imagination. Sometimes imagination can be the most powerful of all attributes of the mind, and I should have allowed my mind to work and see what it would generate. I should have listened to what was being told me by my father-in-law rather than cutting him off and thinking only of coming back out of the cone and onto level ground again. Had I used this creative process of imagination instead of falling back into the most deadly of human sins, laziness, I would have retained a more lasting image of this wonder.

The experience, too, would have given me a greater understanding and appreciation in later years when I witnessed the eruption of neighboring Mt. St. Helens. Like most of the thousands who on that Sunday morning in May 1980 observed a giant gray plume heading north by northeast over the southern Washington farmlands, I did not realize that I was witnessing an event that occurs perhaps once in several lifetimes. Mt. St. Helens was erupting, and I was personally seeing the top of that once cone-shaped mountain self-destruct.

Although I did not fully recognize yet that a geological wonder was taking place before my eyes, I had a professional instinct to run to the newspaper office where I worked and become involved somehow in the excitement. That only became a sickening disappointment. I was not on the crisis team. Even though I worked there, my duties were with the weekly magazine. Becoming involved in the drama of the moment was denied me. I had to settle for second best.

This time, however, I wasted little time in using my imagination. I decided this historic event had to be captured not merely for the daily readers but for generations to follow. It was then I came upon the idea to chronicle the eruption in a book, which was later published and sold beyond all expectations.

The eruption of Mt. St. Helens, which, though in neighboring Washington state, lies only about 45 miles from the Oregon line, has sparked renewed interest in one of Oregon's, and probably one of the Northwest's, most famous volcanos—Mt. Mazama, today filled by Crater Lake.

The calm beauty of Crater Lake gives no hint of the violent forces that originally formed it.

The beginning of the formation of Crater Lake was the eruption of Mt. Mazama about 7,000 years ago. Mt. Mazama, today a dormant volcano, was then one in a group of huge cones that extended along the crest of the Cascade Range from Lassen Peak in Northern California to Mt. Garibaldi near Vancouver, British Columbia. When the mountain exploded and collapsed inward, it created a *caldera* (Spanish for "kettle") or vast crater within the 2,000-foot walls that remained. Snow and rain fell into the hole, gradually filling it and creating the country's deepest lake, at 1,932 feet.

Here are some things to know before you embark on your Crater Lake trip.

Crater Lake is a national park located in southern Oregon. There is a modest entrance fee to the park. It is accessible by highway 138, which connects to I-5 down the Willamette Valley or 97 through central Oregon. However, this is snow country for much of the year beginning in October and sometimes lasting into July. The best time to visit is July, August, and early September. Rim Village, on the edge of the caldera and three miles from park headquarters, is the only area accessible for viewing from mid-October to early June.

Most viewpoints are wheelchair accessible. There is camping on a no-reservation basis from about early June through September, depending on weather. Until Crater Lake Lodge reopens in 1994 or later, there is no overnight inn-type lodging. There are some motel-type cabins spring through fall. Fishing, hiking, and cross-country skiing are permitted but under strictly regulated conditions. There are boat tours from early July to early September.

One warning. A gas station near park headquarters is open only from about Memorial Day to October. During winter months, gas stations are at least 30 miles away. Best to fill up on I-5 or 97 before driving in.

Wolf Creek Inn

A U.S. president slept here; you can, too

When I first came upon Wolf Creek Tavern, it was boarded up, sealed tight, and off limits. Here, in the midst of forests of conglomerations of evergreens and deciduous trees in their bright fall colors, was an abandoned historic jewel. The year was 1978. Wolf Creek Tavern, a relic of a romantic past, had been allowed to fade away, and no one seemed to care. Was Oregon going to lose another leaf of history?

At the time I was editor of *The Oregonian*'s *Northwest* magazine, a supplement that I had started in 1965 and edited and directed to 1982. It was here that I first wrote about the need to save and restore this Oregon landmark.

Wolf Creek is a community about 25 miles north of Grants Pass off I-5. Many years ago, before the turn of the century it was a stagecoach stop for the traveler heading north to Portland or south to San Francisco.

The first commercial lodging here was the Six Bit House, said to be named for the 75-cents-a-night fee when most inns charged a dollar. Six Bit House was built in 1853 beside the wagon road. When the original burned down, a new one was built closer to what is now Wolf Creek.

But Six Bit House was driven out of business by Ben C. Holladay, the pioneer entrepreneur who, at that time, was known as "the stagecoach king." He built the new Wolf Creek Tavern in 1857. Its pillared front balcony was considered a new idea in this region at that time, an inspiration of some of the builders who had been imported from New England.

Among notables who stayed there were U.S. President Rutherford B. Hayes, an overnight visitor in 1880, who signed the guest book, and Jack London, who is reported to have stayed there while he finished writing *The Valley of the Moon*.

By today's standards, stagecoach traveling involved bruising journeys over rough roads and forbidding terrain. The inn was for the traveler of that era a lodge that offered a hot meal, a warm bath, a cozy fire, and clean sheets.

The disappearance of the stagecoach and the arrival of the railroad and later the auto caused the decline of the old hostelry. Not long after Hayes stayed there, the railroad bypassed the old site. The later Pacific Highway brought auto travelers to Wolf Creek, but the present Interstate 5 passes a half-mile from the inn.

The inn was bought at a sheriff's sale in 1955 by W. W. Martin, a Grants Pass businessman. In 1965 it was still open for business, publicized as "the last of the inns built along the Sacramento-to-Portland stagecoach route by Ben Holladay."

In 1973, the building was added to the National Register of Historic Places. However, that year the overnight rooms were closed while the tavern continued to operate as a tourist attraction.

The state bought the building in 1977, and at the time I saw it, in 1978, it appeared to be simply moldering away. But finally the state restored it and reopened it in 1979.

Wolf Creek Inn is one of the most delightful auto stops on I-5. I highly recommend it not only for its historical significance but also for its cuisine, definitely Oregon but with a European flavor.

Tillamook

Where cow is queen and cheese is champion

They used to call it "The Land of Cheese, Trees and Ocean Breeze." It's more. With the improvement of Highway 6 between Portland and Tillamook, it is becoming the fastest route to the ocean.

For many years, Tillamook remained a community known primarily for its Tillamook cheese factory. This Land of Many Waters (the Indian meaning of Tillamook) is becoming one of the prime attractions of the northern coast.

For years I had been driving from Portland to Seaside and Portland to Lincoln City in pursuit of a day in the sea wind. However, one day I had occasion to be an invited speaker in Tillamook. I had planned, rather foolishly, to avoid what I remembered as a tortuous and slow road to Tillamook via Highway 6. The alternatives were to drive south from Seaside or north from Lincoln City on Highway 101. Both approaches, I thought, would be over better road. But then I recalled hearing that Highway 6 had recently undergone major repairs after a rock slide which had sealed the road. Reportedly, the crews had not only repaired the highway but improved it, eliminating many of the slow stretches.

As it turned out, Highway 6 was now a route of easy motoring and scenic pleasure, offering generous views of the beautiful Wilson River.

I was delighted by it. Certainly it will open Tillamook to a greater migration of tourists.

Tillamook got its start as a small farming community. The first settler came to this hidden coastal town in the early 1850s, and soon pioneers discovered the region's rich grassland. It was not hard to figure out that with its many streams (seven to be exact), gentle rain, and mild year-round climate, this was ideal country for raising dairy herds. Soon farmers were acquiring herds of Holstein, Jersey, and Guernsey cows, and in 1894 a Canadian by the name of Peter McIntosh started the fine art of making natural cheddar cheese.

Cheddaring is a cheesemaking process with its roots in fourteenth-century England. It is named for a small town in England, Cheddar, where the process was first developed.

The cheese is made from fresh whole milk. Tillamook cheddar is considered to be the number one selling cheese in the Pacific Northwest. Every year, 40 million pounds of cheese with the legendary Tillamook label are delivered to destinations throughout the world.

In addition to its specialization in agriculture and cheese, the area depends on fishing and timber as sources of income. However, the latest and fastest addition to the local economy is tourism.

Tillamook city faces the Coast Range mountains, its back to the sea. It is only eight miles from the ocean.

If you head south of Tillamook on Highway 101, about two miles out you discover a very large building—actually the largest free-standing wooden structure in the world. (There used to be two buildings, but one burned down in 1992.) The buildings were built during World War II to house a fleet of naval blimps used along the coast to detect Japanese submarine activity.

The blimps were involved in the sinking of what were believed to be two Japanese submarines off Cape Meares. In late May 1943, two blimps, assisted by U.S. Navy sub-chasers and destroyers, dropped several depth charges on the submarines. The Japanese subs are still lying on the ocean floor.

Following the war years, the two hangars were at first converted for use as sawmills but were later leased to other business ventures, such as airship construction.

The remaining building is 300 feet wide, 1,100 feet long, and 195 feet high, large enough to contain seven football fields. It has become a museum open to the public, allowing the curious a peek inside. From there, the imagination should take over.

The entire war defense activity on the West Coast was highly secret, and the public was not told at the time how the Japanese had successfully penetrated our coastal defenses with incendiary bombs. Fortunately, the penetration was not significant, but the Japanese were able to drop some incendiary bombs in hopes of causing a catastrophic forest fire.

It was a bold plan with meager results. One little known tragedy occurred on May 5, 1945, when six children on a picnic in Klamath County were killed by Japanese bombs. These were the only casualties on American soil as a result of enemy action. Twenty gas bombs were found in Klamath County.

The fact that the Japanese did drop bombs on American soil, if it had been made public at the time, could have had grave propaganda consequences.

Having been impressed by the hangar, you can be further dazzled, this time by nature, if you continue driving southward. About seven miles south of Tillamook are numerous coastal waterfalls. The most beautiful, because of its spectacularly rugged descent, is Munson Creek Falls, dropping a dizzying 266 feet over rugged cliffs. A sign off Highway 101 will direct you to a 1.5-mile roadway leading to the parking area and trails. The lower trail is a short, easy walk to the base of the falls, with a picnic area nearby. The upper trail, approachable with a little more effort, will give you a midpoint view of the falls.

Other interesting falls in the county include Nehalem Falls, about eight miles east of Mohler (in this case some miles north of the city of Tillamook); Clarence Creek Falls, about 12 miles east of Beaver; and, for the hiker, Gunaldo Falls, about 11 miles south of Hebo. These are all reached by Highway 101, which in this region swings substantially inland away from the ocean for about 40 miles, rejoining the Pacific at Neskowin.

Enjoy the peace and beauty of this area—a domain settled by early immigrant farmers whose willingness to perform hard work made Tillamook a proud community.

Oregon Coast

The state's favorite play-ground, from placid beach to teetering precipice

I wake up each morning to the sight of a natural barrier of tall firs that still al-lows on a clear day a view of Mt. St. Helens, the volcano. Birds swoop by my window and find their momentary perches on the many evergreens.

Once these evergreens were part of our Forest Park Corridor. Now this corridor has been discovered as a prime site for new housing. Still, it is a quiet neighborhood on the leeward side of the Willamette Heights hillside in Port-land. It is my private hermitage away from the bursting city central core. But even with all this solitude I am still called to the coast, for there are days when the constant sound of the surf breaking off the rocky shoreline can be purging and cleansing.

The Oregon coast admittedly is a great draw for out-of-state tourists, but Oregon people, too, cherish a lifelong affection for it. This affection knows no season. True, the heaviest traffic comes in the sunnier months. But the coast almost never gets extremely cold or hot, so it attracts pilgrims at all seasons. In summer there is more sun and more activity. Yet many adore the winter with its unpredictable storms. Whale watching peaks around Christmas and again in April and May. Spring school vacation, Labor Day, New Year's Day, all send the inland population out to the beach.

In one way Oregon's coast is like other coasts in the U.S. In the summer the ocean cools it; in the winter the ocean warms it. Here the comparison ends. Oregon's coast is unlike others in that it is still wild and wonderful.

When Martin D'Aquilar piloted his frigate Tres Reyes along what was, in 1603, an uncharted coastline, he saw what he described as "majestic bluffs . . . ancient trees and other sights of unparalleled beauty and splendor."

The entire coast today is still a collection of tiny enclaves of unspoiled beauty, and hopefully it will remain that way. Oregon's coast belongs to the people, for more than 350 miles of it is public domain, set aside early in the twentieth century by Governor Oswald West. He knew that some day others would discover this part of Oregon and want to build, build, build.

Everyone is allowed on the beaches and there is no charge. It is all free.

Convenient feeder roads from inland to the coast did not always exist, yet Oregon people always have headed for the coast. From Portland, it used to be an all-day trip with a stop for a picnic lunch on the way, and the traffic was often bumper to bumper.

Nowadays, a beach trip is an easy one-day jaunt from anywhere in western Oregon. Highway 30 takes you from Portland along the meandering Columbia River to Astoria. Highway 26 hits the ocean between Seaside and Cannon Beach, two of the hottest destinations. Or you can branch off and take Highway 6 direct to Tillamook, where the beach cities are more rustic and old-timey.

Interstate 5 connects with coastal feeder highways all the way to the California border. Highway 18 hits the central coast, where Lincoln City and Newport are the big tourist vortices. You can also peel off I-5 at Albany to hit Newport directly. From Eugene, Highway 126 connects with Florence, opening the whole palette of south central beach towns. Then there's Highway 38, taking you to Winchester Bay and Highway 42 to Bandon and Coos Bay. Now, you're really into southern coastal country, which is dramatically different from the north.

Actually, all tourists owe themselves at least once a continuous trip down coastal Highway 101, with side trips, from Astoria to Brookings and perhaps on into Crescent City, California. In this book you can sample the whole menu, then decide which destination best suits your needs, prevailing mood, and pocketbook.

Come with me as we enjoy the coast from the most northern tip to its southern shores, where there are trees predating the white man's civilization, streams abundant with salmon, and forests alive with deer, elk, and bear.

For the complete north-to-south tour, the best starting point is Highway 30 through northwest Portland, following the meandering lower Columbia River to its mouth and the maritime city of Astoria. Astoria claims to be the oldest permanent American settlement west of the Rockies dating from 1811, when fur traders established a post there.

This is one of my favorite stops when I take Highway 30. Astoria has by far one of the most breathtaking views of the Columbia River, and few cities on the West Coast have comparable beauty. Oh, yes, there is San Francisco,

Seattle, and Vancouver, B.C., but Astoria is an undiscovered gem, and I think the majority of the population there prefer it that way.

Until recently, the only ethnic diversity in Astoria came from the Tongue Point Naval Base and the subsequent Job Corps. Most of the people were sturdy Finns, who at first came here to work as fishermen and lumbermen. The Finns are a deeply reserved people who keep to themselves and are especially reticent with outsiders. This was impressed on me most forcibly when I had to interview a Finnish family near Astoria. At no time were they the least bit discourteous. But they were people who carefully chose their words, and to say they spoke with spartan brevity would be an understatement. Sometimes, my conversation with them would be merely a monologue, with me doing all the talking and them simply looking at me.

Astoria is not a beach at all, but a harbor, yet there are some must-see attractions there. Most obligatory is a climb up the interior 164 steps of the Astoria Column on Coxcomb Hill. The 125-foot tower, built in 1926, affords a view of the lower Columbia River, the Pacific Ocean, and as far as the Mt. St. Helens volcano on a clear day. The exterior contains a spiral mural depicting the area's history.

If you're particularly interested in things maritime, the Columbia River Maritime Museum is open daily with live demonstrations of rope making and net mending on weekends.

Some six miles south of Astoria, a little off Highway 101, you find the Fort Clatsop National Memorial. Here is a replica of the stockade fort the Lewis and Clark expedition built in 1905 to weather over the winter. Your first reaction may be: Were these people really small enough to fit into those little buildings? Yes, they were. Americans have been getting progressively bigger. If you visit the fort on a rainy day, you can appreciate what this shelter meant to the explorers through the damp, chilly winter.

At about 18 miles south of Astoria you encounter your first genuine beach resort town. It is upscale Gearhart, a kind of "suburb" of Seaside just to the south. Gearhart has a history of being somewhat staid and high ticket, but old locals like to tell of some famous parties supposedly hosted years ago by the Hollywood film actor, Tab Hunter. Actually, I never met anyone who claimed to have attended one of those parties, so it may just be part of local legend. Gearhart lists two golf courses, the first of many sprinkled along the Oregon shore.

I can't leave Gearhart without romanticizing a bit about the "Old

Gearhart" and the posh and high-nosed reputation it had before the "others" came. At the center of town was a marvelous old lodge, the Gearhart Hotel, where one could enter alone and within minutes meet a half dozen or more local personalities whose magnetism was unforgettable.

One such personality was John Osborne. He owned the place. He not only liked to talk to everyone but loved to hold forth if there was a member of the press in the crowd. John Osborne introduced me to more people than I can remember. It was John Osborne who introduced me to Bill Holmstrom, the state senator from Astoria who had a dream about building a bridge across the mouth of the Columbia. Holmstrom, Osborne, and I and a few other locals spent many a night sitting in the Old Gearhart Hotel bar and dreaming big dreams about what Oregon would be like someday when it was recognized for more than its rain and trees. Well, it did happen.

Unfortunately, one of the first changes was the demolition of the old Gearhart Hotel to make way for a new trend—the condominium. And the advent of the condominium meant the demise of the social gathering place where you could retreat from the storm of daily living and be among new-found friends. The residents of Gearhart do like the way things are now, but some mourn the passing of more intimate times when storytelling and a drink with a new friend or an old one were the joys of coastal seclusion.

If Gearhart is somewhat stolid, Seaside definitely is not. It is the clattering, clanging kaleidoscope of modern beach cities. Seaside was Oregon's first seashore resort, and for those who like civilized excitement along with beach amenities it remains the ultimate. Lewis and Clark supposedly stopped here, evaporating sea water in a rock cairn to get salt. The intrepid explorers never would recognize it today.

At the heart of Seaside is what the Seaside Chamber of Commerce likes to call "the million dollar walk." It's Broadway, extending east and west through the heart of the city to an elevated turnaround jutting out over the wide sandy beach. On this walk, the visitor passes gift shops, restaurants, candy stores, clothing shops, a shooting gallery, popcorn, pizza, arcade games, and even carnival rides. All this boisterous action makes it a favorite hangout for kids and teens.

Tooling along south from Seaside, you actually have to make what appears to be a turnoff to the right to stay on 101; otherwise you're back on Highway 26 headed for Portland again.

Soon, you encounter Cannon Beach, probably to Oregon people the most famous resort town of all. It is full of artists, writers, musicians, actors. There's a live theater, galleries, cute little shops of all kinds, restaurants. Unfortunately, it is essentially a one-street town, Hemlock Street, and in the peak season the crowds can approach excess. However, it's a well-behaved town, not noisy or rowdy, and if you have trouble finding parking on the main street, there are back streets available.

The big annual event of Cannon Beach is the Sandcastle Contest, which usually comes in late spring. Genuine artists from distant states come to compete, mainly for the joy of showing their skills. A warning: Don't arrive late in the day of the contest and expect anything but a traffic jam. Arrive early, preferably the night before. The time of the contest depends on the tide, and sometimes the contest reaches its peak in the fairly early morning hours.

Just north of Cannon Beach lies Ecola State Park, featuring old growth forest, high cliffs over the ocean, and sandy coves with volcanic rock outcroppings, reached by trails extending downward. Just south of Cannon Beach is Haystack Rock, 235 feet high and a bird sanctuary. Although it is surrounded by water at high tide, at low tide it is possible to climb around the base through some rather kinky rock formations and tidepools alive with little marine animals and plants.

Hemlock Street leads south from Cannon Beach and eventually rejoins 101, meanwhile taking you through some charming little settlements hugging the ocean shore.

About 10 miles south of Cannon Beach you come upon one of the true jewels of the Oregon park system, Oswald West State Park, named for the governor who preserved the beaches for public domain. The park contains almost 2,500 acres, much of which is rain forest and a lot of which is beach. There are some overnight campsites at Short Sands Beach. Getting into the park requires walking a few blocks but is well worth the effort.

As you continue south you begin climbing up from sea level until you are skirting Neahkahnie Mountain at about 700 feet elevation. Here is romance, mystery, intrigue. Indians supposedly related stories of a beached Spanish galleon and buried boxes of treasure at the foot of the mountain. Strangely marked rocks have been found, supposedly directions to the treasure. Alas, many decades of searching have turned up some artifacts but nothing valuable.

Now ensues one of the most delightful legs of this odyssey, as 101 winds through a series of curves that sometimes take you deep into forest land and sometimes bring you out in view of the ocean.

This 40-mile stretch, ending in Tillamook, represents tranquil beach experience at its best. In this entire stretch there is no superhighway feeding in, bringing hordes of day trippers. Yet each little community has its conveniences, comfortable lodgings, interesting dining, and exquisite scenery.

Because this stretch is so close to sea level, the highway is flanked on the inland side by a series of lakes, most of which have little or no shoreline, tend to be somewhat reedy, and can actually project a feeling of brooding moroseness. But the beach all along here cannot be surpassed. It is wide and level and seems to extend forever.

Suddenly this stretch ends in more curves and woods, and you're facing the wide expanse of Tillamook Bay. A winding road takes you around the east end into the colorful little fishing village of Garibaldi, perched on a few hills overlooking the bay.

Deep-sea charter fishing and sightseeing are big industries in Garibaldi today. Deep-sea anglers bring back rock fish, halibut, ling cod, and salmon, all delicious eating. Garibaldi was a major lumber shipping port and a bustling mill town until the fateful Tillamook Burn forest fire in the 1930s, a conflagration that destroyed billions of board feet of timber.

Between Garibaldi and the next little town, Bay City, lies the Miami River, renowned for its trout fishing. Stream angling is one of the attractions that lures many who might never consider a walk on the sandy beach. All along the coastline there are rivers that run into bays or long stretches of tidewater where trout, steelhead and even salmon bring anglers back to the same grounds year after year.

Looking across Tillamook Bay, one can see the ghost town of Bay Ocean. This is a sand spit that developers many decades ago touted as Oregon's premier resort area. A number of homes were built on the spit, but the ocean was not to be denied. Storms beat without mercy at the fragile sand, and at one time the ocean completely severed the spit from the mainland. Eventually Bay Ocean was totally abandoned, but today you might still see some remains of home foundations anchored there so hopefully, so long ago.

You pass the Kilchis River, another favorite trout stream, just before reaching the Tillamook County Cheese Factory just outside Tillamook. The factory welcomes visitors on self-guided tours. Nearby is another cheese factory, the Blue Heron French, where wine tasting is also offered.

Tillamook has already been described in its own chapter.

At Tillamook you can either continue on Highway 101 or leave it for some 38 miles and opt for the Three Capes Scenic Loop. Take the long way. Head west out of Tillamook on Third Street, and at about seven miles out you will come to a fork in the road. The left fork leads directly to Netarts on 101; the right fork (the one you want) will give you the entire Three Capes experience.

Are you missing something by not continuing on 101 as it swings inland? Yes, it's a question of priorities. If you have the time, perhaps you could try it both ways. The inland route heads upmountain, passing through colorful Beaver on the Nestucca River and Hebo, once a crossroads for travelers to the coast. Much of the route, especially around Cloverdale, is through restful rural back country, with weathered fences, lowing cattle, white-painted barns, and similar bucolic attractions. But the beach on this route is out of reach.

If you take the Three Capes Loop, you'll first pass the inland end of ill-fated Bay Ocean sand spit and then continue on north to the lighthouse at Cape Meares. Opened in 1890, the lighthouse is one of only two eight-sided lighthouses in the country. It was decommissioned in 1963 and replaced by an automated beacon in the same area. Now it's a state day park. As you might expect, the view is superb.

Besides the lighthouse, Cape Meares is noted for one strange tree, called the Octopus Tree. It's a venerable Sitka spruce, with limbs three to five feet thick that branch out close to the ground and seem to be writhing in various directions.

Continuing south on the loop road from Cape Meares, you encounter one of the most pleasureable stretches of ocean front in the entire state. Along it lies a string of small, quiet beach communities. The contrast to bustling Tillamook can be startling, and it lasts pretty much until you get back onto Highway 101 near Pacific City. Yes, there are new structures here and there, but the atmosphere is one of old-timey charm. The pace is measured, nay, downright sluggish compared to the frenetic excitement of Seaside or the sophisticated elan of Cannon Beach.

Oceanside is the first such little burg. A high dark rock promontory juts into the ocean just north of Oceanside, giving the whole area an atmosphere of gothic mystery, particularly when misty fog enshrouds the area, as it frequently does. The promontory offers a marvelous jump-off point for hang gliding. At one point it had a tunnel drilled through it, but the tunnel was finally closed because of the danger of falling rocks (although there have been frequent pressures to reopen it). Even more exciting was a circular wooden staircase, weatherbeaten and creaky, climbing from the beach to the top of the cliff for a scary view down its steep backside. Winter storms swept away the bottom of the staircase, although for years you could climb the lower cliff and still get onto the spiraling steps. Finally, years after being officially condemned as unsafe, the staircase was removed.

Two miles south of Oceanside is a similar community, Netarts, facing a long sand spit which forms Netarts Bay. A road here cuts back to Tillamook, should you discover you've forgotten something like buying a block of that exceptional cheese.

Continuing south on the loop road, you encounter the Whiskey Creek Fish Hatchery, where 100,000 spring Chinook salmon get their starts in life.

Soon you reach the second of the three capes, Lookout, extending a mile and a half into the ocean. The forested trail out to the end of the cape offers spectacular views. Cape Lookout has a modern state park with overnight camping by reservation.

Finally you reach Cape Kiwanda, rather a strange-looking cape, especially compared to the woodsy Meares and Lookout. It's mostly sandstone, not very steep but stretching out further than Meares or Lookout. My own feeling about Kiwanda is, here is one weird cape. The erosion of wind and waves on the soft sandstone has created bizarre shapes reminiscent of gargoyles on a Romanesque cathedral or possibly provocative images in a Fellini film.

Just south of Cape Kiwanda is Pacific City, a cute little oceanfront village on the Nehalem River bay where fishermen still push squat little boats called dories out into the surf. Here you will find a road joining up with Highway 101 again. But before leaving this area, you must cross over to the ocean side of the bay and visit Nestucca Spit.

Today, Nestucca Spit has been renamed Bob Straub State Park, in honor of another more recent governor who worked hard to retain beach access for the public. This place always gives me an eerie feeling. It is, after all, a sand spit, like the doomed Bay Ocean spit although not so exposed. On the landward side of the spit a number of homes and buildings have been erected. But the ocean keeps wearing away the land, creeping inward, seeking to swallow up these buildings. Can the residents drive it back? They couldn't at Bay Ocean.

Now, you've rejoined Highway 101 and you continue southward through acres of evergreen trees with occasional glimpses of a distant ocean. Eventually you will reach Otis Junction, where Highway 18 from Portland (including 22 from Salem) feeds its busy traffic into Highway 101. You're at the gateway to the central Oregon coast, with its multitude of beaches, ocean-front towns, and parklands.

The north central coast, more or less contained within Lincoln County and extending from just south of Cascade Head to Yachats, draws many native residents and tourists. Why? Because they want to go not to "the coast" but to "the beach." And this section of the state is dominated by long, wide, easily accessible sandy beaches, washed by the Great Mother of Waters, the Pacific Ocean, punctuated by rocky headlands, dotted with intriguing tidepools, and caressed by placid inlets.

Just south of Otis Junction is Lincoln City. Today it is a major commercial strip, but back in the 1950s it was a scattering of small towns and communities strung along Highway 101, butting almost cheek-by-jowl, each with its own agenda and priorities. The result was the inevitable hodgepodge of fire control, law enforcement, zoning, and all the other modern governmental mechanisms. Civic leaders sensed the need to create some kind of unity, and in the mid-1960s the five communities banded together to form long, thin Lincoln City. They were, north to south, Oceanlake, Delake, Nelscott, Taft, and Cutler City—a strip seven and a half miles long and in some places not much more than a block wide.

The beach along Lincoln City is not only splendid but varied. In some places, you can step out of your auto and onto the sand. In others, high bluffs overlook what seem almost deserted stretches of sand. Some areas have a background of driftwood logs to add to the interest. In other places, there are tidepools, jutting rocks, or trickling creeks. There are numerous public access points, some of them wheelchair accessible.

In northern Lincoln City, D River, billed as "the world's shortest river," flows out of Devil's Lake, which immediately adjoins the highway. Here is a lake with a multitude of recreational possibilities both on top of and beneath the water, but with a somewhat tortured and unusual recent history. This history led to the introduction of a fish festival in which the fish so honored is not caught, cooked, eaten or even memorialized in picture or painting.

Being a lake with a sluggish inflow and outflow, Devil's Lake became over the years clogged with a pernicious water weed, milfoil. At its worst points, the milfoil reached the surface, making large areas impossible to penetrate by boat or swimmer.

Faced with the eventual total loss of the lake as a recreational facility, the city decided it must take some action. In the mid-1980s, a fish called the White Amur grass carp was trucked in from an Arkansas fish hatchery and introduced into the lake. This is a species that purportedly relishes the flavor of milfoil.

When introduced, the grass carp were small fingerlings, but as they grew they chomped and chomped ever more effectively at the milfoil until the lake was sufficiently cleared so that recreation could return to it. In gratitude, the community in 1986 founded the annual September Grass Carp Festival.

The Taft district, in southern Lincoln City, is pretty much self-contained as a town, and has a more rustic atmosphere than other districts. The big beach attraction is the Bay Front, a long sweep of land facing Siletz Bay.

On the opposite shore of the bay is a long sand spit called Salishan Spit. This has become an area of privately owned homes protected from the madding crowd by a security gate.

Alas for the spit, it is not protected from the inexorable ocean. It faces the same erosion problems that wiped out Bay Ocean many years ago. In the early 1970s, some Salishan homes toppled into the sea. Heavy infusions of riprap, a favorite term of the Army Engineers for piles of boulders, have helped the spit hold its own in recent years. At least one home on the spit was built on stilts, apparently to allow a rampant ocean simply to flow underneath. Since the spit is a private enclave, very little news of its current condition has been circulated.

At Taft, the bay shore is open to the public and is an area of recreational delights. At low tide, the bay becomes shallow. It is common to observe seals basking on sand bars or frolicking in the shallow water.

Facing the bay is the pier from which one can fish or drop crab traps, often with surprising success. Indeed, crabbing at Taft with my friends John and Kina Armstrong, back in the 1950s, was my first experience of the Oregon coast. I remember how I lowered a circular metal basket containing a bountiful supply of bait into the waters directly below the pier. After some waiting, not too long I recall, I hoisted up the basket. It was filled with feasting Dungeness crabs, all sizes within the legal limit.

Tossing that live catch into boiling water was not easy. My wife described it as a "cold-blooded act." But the feast of fresh crab, cold beer, and chips, accompanied by good company, the sight of the ocean, and the fresh air were memorable.

From Taft, 101 crosses the Siletz River, technically past the rather anonymous community of Cutler City. From there it skirts Siletz Bay, large but very shallow in spots. At low tide, it can become a patchwork of sand bars, mud flats, and grassy marshes. From here, Highway 101 swings inland, just out of sight of the ocean, for some eight miles. The wide beach continues on, interrupted just south of Lincoln Beach by Fishing Rock but not disappearing entirely until it reaches Fogarty Creek.

Fogarty Creek is a charming state park, a well-loved stopover for day use. Inland from the highway lies a woodsy picnic area. From there you walk a creekside trail under a highway bridge to a beach studded with rock formations.

When I drive by Fogarty Creek, I can remember the day I spent on that beach 30 years ago with my wife and my two small children, who were then in preschool. The kids wanted to jump into a big tidepool, maybe four feet deep and ten feet wide. It was a hot day, the September sun was blistering the sand, and the pool looked refreshing and inviting.

"Go ahead, jump into it!" I can still hear my wife's words as I write this. She is gone now: she left us many years ago when she could no longer fight the disease which she called "The Big C." What remains is the memory of that afternoon at Fogarty Creek when she told the children, "Go ahead and jump in! You will never forget this as long as you live."

My daughter jumped in. My son also took his turn, and both of them shared in the joy. I watched nearby, not interfering, not making cautionary gestures as I often did, because something told me to sit this one out and just let it be. And to this day whenever I drive by Fogarty Creek I can still hear her voice and the happy giggles of my little daughter and son jumping into that natural shallow pool in the rocks along the water's edge of the white sandy beach at Fogarty Creek. That to me is the Oregon coast. It belongs to me now.

Below Fogarty Creek, the beach eventually disappears into rock cliffs, beginning the longest stretch of beachless coastline in Lincoln County. Even in this stretch, however, there are little sections of "pocket" beach, some of them not accessible to the public.

From here southward, the coastline takes a wilder, more primitive character. Low-lying rock formations have become molded into tortured shapes through millenia of assault from the battering ocean. In some places, the waves rebound upward against the rock headlands to spout high into the air.

Highway 101 first returns to the ocean at Depoe Bay. So popular is this area that there is more parking lot than actual town, and even then the lot is sometimes full.

The town itself is just one building deep, east of the highway and parking lot. On the west side of the highway is a glass-enclosed viewing room where one can marvel at the untamed grandeur of the wild Pacific Ocean without even mussing one's hair.

Depoe Bay calls itself the world's smallest harbor, and who's to argue? In times past, the entrance was only 20 feet wide, a mere crack between evil-looking basalt headlands, navigable only at high tide. In mid-century, the Army Corps of Engineers enlarged the entrance to 50 feet at its widest, 5 feet deep at its shallowest. It's still a tricky passage, with boats almost seeming to edge their way through.

Depoe Bay harbor, narrow as it may be, is a popular start point for deep sea fishing expeditions and whale-watching trips.

Whale watching is one of the favorite off-season pastimes on the coast. Every year the gray whale summers far north in the Bering sea, then swims south to winter in warm, shallow lagoons off the coast of Baja, California. They pass southward around Christmas and move north again between late March and early May. They can be seen at numerous places along the coast, especially where capes jut out into the ocean.

The whales pass quite close to the shore but can be seen better from boats. These whales are fearless because, full-grown, they are huge—often 50 feet long. Being fearless, they allow boats to come quite close, although there is some evidence that too much familiarity annoys the whales. They are believed to be passing close to land to keep their bearings and also, possibly, because they are naturally curious.

In the family of whales, the gray is the plain-looking sister. She has a body like a long cigar and a long, small head that tapers down to a point almost like a beak. Her body is covered with irregular bumps which look like huge warts.

This is not the whale you picture when you see Monstro The Whale in Walt Disney's *Pinocchio*, or the sleek little whale that kisses the pretty lady at

Sea World. Yet she has her own type of beauty and deserves to be recognized for the great gentle beast she is.

Whale watching has its own specialized lingo, with words like "breaching" and "fluke." It's a fascinating subject in itself, and most coastal book stores and gift shops carry detailed resource material.

About two miles south of Depoe Bay you can turn into the Otter Crest Loop and get back to ocean viewing. Here are some memorable viewpoints, one of them from the aptly named Cape Foulweather, another from Devil's Punchbowl. The punchbowl is a natural bowl formed when the sandstone roof over two adjoining sea caves collapsed. This left a fissure which, at high tide, the ocean fills with churning, foaming waves.

South of the Otter Crest Loop, Highway 101 descends again and moves closer to the ocean as the sandy beach reappears. The beach will continue now, with a few minor breaks, until Lincoln County comes to an end south of Yachats.

Soon, you find yourself in Newport, crossroads of the north central coast, where Highway 101 meets Highway 20 connecting inland to Corvallis, Albany, and I-5.

Newport's slogan is "more to do here," and it is no exaggeration. But while in Lincoln City and Depoe Bay, it's all in one place, in Newport it's in a number of different places, making transportation by motor or bicycle essential.

First, there is a full-scale city. Then, there is a beach, a very good beach. There is also a fishing port, a mind-boggling new aquarium, and a pretty park for picnicking—all of them separated by substantial geography.

Coming in on Highway 101, you begin passing through the city. Soon, around 15th Street, you reach a turnoff to Nye Beach. This is a separate beach complex, a compact parking lot surrounded by stores, shops, and restaurants, with a ramp leading onto the sand. In the same area is a Performing Arts Center. Nye Beach is like a little self-contained community.

Back on 101, you soon reach the park, high overlooking Yaquina Bay.

Even if you skip the beach and park, you must visit the Bay Front. This is a combination of working fishing port and tourist attraction. Among the canneries, boat moorages, and crab pots are interspersed all sorts of restaurants and shops with that old-timey flavor. The scent of fish and salt water hangs in the air. A refreshing breeze wafts across the bayside walkway.

Here you'll find the original Mo's restaurant, where you crowd into a tiny alcove to savor clam chowder and grilled or deep fried ocean fish, served on tables made from the old wooden hatch covers of long-forgotten ships. The actor Paul Newman hung out here during production of the filming of Ken Kesey's novel, *Sometimes a Great Notion*. Mo's became so famous as a result that it opened branches in other locations.

The Bay Front also contains a privately operated marine life attraction, Undersea Gardens. You descend below the bay surface to find yourself surrounded by more than 5,000 live specimens of sea life. Tour guides narrate a performance every few minutes, illustrated in the water by a scuba diver who picks up or points to the specimens.

The peak experience in Newport today is the new (opened in May, 1992) Oregon Coast Aquarium. To reach it, you cross the Yaquina Bay Bridge and drive onto a peninsula, for your most dramatic sea life spectacle on the entire Oregon coast. It was built at a cost of $24 million and designed specifically as a tourist lure, with substantial paid admission price. It's worth it.

The aquarium combines both indoor and outdoor exhibits, all aiming to re-create natural habitats. "Sandy Shores" has leopard sharks darting among pier pilings. "Rocky Shores" finds waves crashing over a rocky beach, host waters for strange looking fish, starfish and shellfish.

Outdoors, a series of pools, both tidepools and deeper lagoons, lead the visitor through a variety of exhibits. Seals and sea lions frolic in one pool before an underwater window. In a coastal cave lurks a giant Pacific octopus. Tufted puffin, rhinoceros auklets, murres, and other sea birds perch atop a 30-foot cliff, to dive into a pool nine feet deep. This is billed as the largest open-air seabird aviary in North America.

Stars of the show are the sea otters. Everything in the aquarium is originally native to the Oregon coast, although the otters have been extinct on the coast since 1911. These otters were not plucked from a happy and wild existence. They are rehabilitated victims of the gigantic Alaskan oil spill.

If you can see through or over the crowds that always surround the otter pool, you'll crack up at the antics of these natural comedians. To keep them amused, the staff gives the otters big blocks of ice to chew on. Even when asleep, the otters are funny. They float around the pool on their backs like so many driftwood logs, occasionally bumping gently into one another and even forming floating clumps of two or more furry bodies lazily drifting here and there.

Adjacent to the aquarium is the older, free, Hatfield Marine Sciences Center, with many fine exhibits of the more conventional aquarium type.

Some parts of Yaquina Bay are so shallow that the tide flats regularly emerge for good clamming

So, the problem with Newport is not a lack of things to do, but a lack of time to do it all, especially on a one-day trip.

South of Newport, Highway 101 runs close to the sandy beach again, then cuts inland to cross Alsea Bay into Waldport.

Now, the environment becomes much different. The beach is wide and splendid, but the shoreline is much less built up. Most of the houses are on large lots, within woodsy settings or framed by hummocky beach grass. Many of the residential streets are unpaved and winding. The feeling becomes one of more natural unspoiled beauty, a feeling which trickled away somewhere north of Lincoln City and only now has become revived.

Yachats is more of the same uncrowded atmosphere, although by now the beach disappears again. South of Yachats, Cape Perpetua juts into the Pacific. It's said to be the highest point on the Oregon coast. On the cape is a highly developed visitor center, with 18 miles of forest trails, tide pools, interpretive features, all operated by the U.S. Forest Service.

Nearby are Indian middens, a polite name for ancient garbage dumps. In this case, the garbage consists of huge mounds of seashells, now covered over by grass. It is estimated that these sea shell creatures were eaten by the Indians a thousand years ago.

Driving along the rocky basaltic coastline, you encounter Heceta Head, where a lighthouse was first installed in 1894 but now runs as an automated gadget. The head marks approximately the north-south midpoint of the Oregon coast.

South a little further lies the privately operated Sea Lion Caves. An elevator takes you down to a huge grotto, where sea lions bellow and yelp. These are big sea lions, with ears. The bulls can weigh up to 1,500 pounds. The sea lions live here year round on what is said to be the only mainland rookery between California and the Bering Sea. Normally, sea lions hang out on offshore rocks. These sea lions seem to pay absolutely no attention to the gawking spectators and perhaps don't even see them.

Now Highway 101 swings inland, and with good reason. You are entering a totally different world. It is the south central coast, where you find yourself surrounded by the mystery, the romance, of dune country.

You realize you're in a strange new environment before you ever get to Florence. About eight miles north of Florence you begin to see dunes, and about five miles north of the city you encounter the Darlingtonia Botanical Wayside.

If Darlingtonia doesn't ring the memory bell, don't be surprised. It's a plant not commonly found, and it is often labeled with other names—pitcher plant, cobra plant, cobra lily. What's unusual about the cobra lily is that it's carnivorous, eats meat, specifically insects. This wayside contains a spooky bog full of Darlingtonia. No, you don't have to descend into the bog to see this chilling dance of doom as insects are lured into passages from which there is no escape. There are walkways overlooking the bog.

On to Florence, at the mouth of the Siuslaw River—a logging and fishing town but one which delights in welcoming tourists. There's an Old Town near the north ramp of the Siuslaw River Bridge, reminiscent in a smaller way of the Bay Front at Newport. It's an easy living kind of town, with as many as half the permanent residents in retirement.

Florence has the advantage of being the terminus of Highway 126 to Eugene and Springfield, making it handy for University of Oregon students who want to hop over to the coast for a day. In the surrounding area are all kinds of opportunities for fishing, hiking, clamming, and crabbing. Rivers, lakes, tide flats, and marshes all are within easy reach. Seals and sea lions make frequent appearances, and in the winter, swans inhabit nearby marshes. Some of the whitest sand dunes you'll ever see rise on the south side of the bay.

The big topic of conversation here is the dunes. Florence is the gateway to the Oregon Dunes National Recreation Area, a strip of dunes which extends more than 40 miles to just north of the neighbor cities of North Bend and Coos Bay. From Florence, Highway 101 juts inland and doesn't return to the coast until Port Orford far to the south, although there are access roads into the dunes at various points and there are scenic loops.

If you're simply driving or bicycling through this area, 40 miles can seem like a lot of dunes, since they shut off any view of the ocean and frequently much of any view inland as well. They are not at all like the endless barren dunes of *Lawrence of Arabia*, although there are some areas with this stark sort of landscape. Many of the dunes areas have large hummocks of grass. There are also dead trees poking up through the sand, like some white petrified forest buried in by shifting sands. There are marshes, some of them populated with that unattractive weed, skunk cabbage.

If you really want to experience dunes country, many attractive possibilities lie before you. The area boasts excellent sandy beaches, freshwater lakes, hiking trails, ponds, and estuaries. The protected reserve covers 14,000 acres of dunes, some more than 500 feet high. In some places, the reserve extends as much as four miles inland. Because the area is protected, wildlife abounds. Blacktail deer, coyote, bobcats, all are seen frequently. More than 200 species of birds have been counted, including the osprey and the bald eagle.

The dunes of this area were formed over many eons. Sandstone near the shore and in the Coast Range mountains became eroded, and the silt was carried to the sea by coastal rivers. From there, the ocean took the silt, ground it even finer, and washed it back onto the mainland. As it dried, the winds took over, scattering it and remolding it into ever-changing shapes.

Dune areas usually start near the beach with a foredune, a hump of sand which in this section of the coast blocks off any view of the ocean. The foredune is hummocky with grass, and fairly stable.

Further inland is a "deflation zone," so-called because the action of the winds on the dry sand tends to scour the surface below the water table level. This results in myriad lakes (32 within this recreation area) and marshes, often with lush vegetation. Out of the deflation zone, the dunes can take a variety of forms, with different name designations such as *traverse dunes*, *oblique dunes*, and *parabola dunes*.

In many cases, the lakes were formed because the buildup of sand prevented the outflow of streams to the ocean. As a result, the lakes backed up, often taking strange shapes, and their outflow often is underground, seeping through the sand.

Three miles south of Florence lies Jesse M. Honeyman State Park, 522 acres of sand dunes, lakes, and rhododendron-filled forests.

About 10 miles south of Florence between the south end of Siltcoos Lake and the north finger of Tahkenitch Lake is an Oregon Dunes Overlook. At Tahkenitch Lake, you regain a feeling of closeness to the ocean.

The most idyllic of reveries finds one sitting in a tiny boat on Lake Tahkenitch, in the late afternoon of a warm, end-of-summer day, fishing line out. Overhead, a few cottony clouds stretch across the deep blue canvas of the sky. The very air seems lush, filled with meaning.

An occasional flying insect hums past, and dark birds weave restlessly over the quiet water. There is no need to be concerned about anything, to take any action, to feel any hurry, to rush any decision. Can there be a distant sound falling on the ear? Yes, an easy rattle of rowlocks, a languid splash of oars. From around a little bend drifts a weathered boat bearing Henry David Thoreau, far from his beloved Walden Pond.

The northern section of the Oregon Dunes National Recreation Area ends soon after you leave Tahkenitch Lake, at Winchester Bay. The southern section picks up south of Winchester Bay, ending at the north spit of Coos Bay.

Salmon Harbor, on Winchester Bay, is billed as the largest sports fishing harbor on the coast. You can leave 101 here for a three-mile tour which takes you along the bay to wide beaches, a coastal visitor center and the Umpqua lighthouse. This side trip leads you past an enormous stretch of dunes, some among the highest in the entire preserve. This is also a preferred whale watching vantage point, with the curious gray whales occasionally sticking their elongated noses right into the river mouth.

Back off the loop and onto 101 south of Salmon Harbor, the highway swings well inland again, skirting a number of lakes, large and small, until it reaches Coos Bay and the side-by-side cities of North Bend and Coos Bay. The dunes recreational area ends at this point, and the wide sandy beaches disappear for some distance, to be replaced by rugged coastline. Here is the end of what is generally known as the "south central coast" and the beginning of the "south coast."

Coos Bay-North Bend constitutes the largest metropolitan center on the coast and in the heyday of logging was called the largest lumber-shipping port in the world. Now you begin to encounter myrtlewood shops. Myrtlewood comes from a tree common to the south coast and (according to local promoters) only one other place in the world, the "Holy Land." It is multi-grained and polishes to a high gloss.

At Coos Bay you can leave Highway 101 for a sojourn westward on the Cape Arago Highway through Charleston, a quaint fishing village in a protected neck of Coos Bay where there are sport fishing and deep-sea rubberneck tours.

From Charleston, you can take a scenic side trip road to the Cape Arago lighthouse, Sunset Bay, and Shore Acres Historical Gardens. (This does require eventually doubling back to Charleston to continue southward.) Shore Acres is a 743-acre park on the shoreline, once a summer home for Louis J. Simpson. The mansion originally at the park no longer exists, but the restored gardens include a glass-enclosed observation shelter on the former mansion site. Thirty varieties of rhododendrons grow here, along with dozens of different trees and shrubs from around the world. The garden has received landscape design awards, and bird watching is exceptional.

Doubling back to Charleston, you follow Seven Devils Road to pass the South Slough National Estuarine Reserve. This very large slough drops southward near the mouth of Coos Bay. A feature of the slough is the presence of major oyster beds, with the Qualman Oyster Farms located in the Joe Ney slough, branching off the South Slough.

All the oysters in Coos Bay are privately owned "immigrants," being cultivated from oyster seed bought from Japan, Washington State, and Canada. The bay water is not warm enough for infant oysters to survive, so they come here when they have attained sufficient maturity. These oysters relax in South Slough for 24 to 30 months, but they do not produce pearls, so poaching would not be too profitable.

South Slough is an estuary, meaning a place where rivers meet the sea and fresh water mixes with salt water. This can create an environment where many types of plants and animals thrive. Most estuaries are spoiled by towns and cities on their shores, but South Slough has escaped this development and is preserved close to its natural state.

About 27 miles south of Coos Bay, Seven Devils Road rejoins Highway 101. Wide sandy beach makes a brief reappearance, only to thin out again as 101 reaches Bandon on the Coquille River. From here on, for some distance, "pocket beaches" are the rule.

Bandon might well have been named Phoenix, for it has risen from the ashes, not once, but twice. The first time was in 1914; the second (well within the memory of many residents) was in 1936. The surrounding country was overgrown with a plant known as oily gorse, and when fire got started in the gorse, it became almost impossible to extinguish. The 1936 fire had residents backed up to the ocean to survive.

Once a lumber town, Bandon has become Bandon-By-The-Sea and calls itself "the storm-watching capital of the world." Tourism is the main thrust of local business, and a thriving art colony gives the town a bohemian atmosphere.

Bandon has been highly successful in selling itself as a tourist attraction. Even the local Coquille Indians cooperate with an annual salmon bake in July. Since cranberry bogs are one of the big local industries, there is a cranberry festival and there are regular tours of the bogs. An historic Old Town adds to the local color.

There is a beach loop which connects with two state parks, Face Rock and Bullards Beach. Unique along the ocean front are sea stacks, needles of rock jutting upward. From here for some distance southward, the sea stacks become a characteristic feature of the seascape.

There is a highly acclaimed hike from Bandon south to Fourmile Creek, about 8.5 miles. This starts among some of the most spectacular rock needles, continuing along a wide, sandy beach deserted except for birds and the occasional hiker. To the east are visible empty dunes, silent lakes, hushed marshlands.

At times, attractive beaches appear along here, but their presence can be deceptive. Many spots show beach at low tide but at high tide the beach vanishes, leaving any hapless hiker stranded against sheer high cliffs.

From here, 101 stays pretty far inland, although there are access roads to the coast. One road leads to Floras Lake State Park, another to Cape Blanco, where there is a lighthouse. Cape Blanco at one time was called the furthest point west in the contiguous United States, but now it is argued it may only be second most western.

At Port Orford, you're back next to the ocean again. This is a natural harbor, with the town overlooking the sea from a marine shelf. The city is noted for myrtlewood and also the Port Orford cedar, highly prized as a decorative wood. There is also an active trade in diving for sea urchins, the odd sea creature whose innards are highly prized as an aphrodisiac in Japan.

The drive from Port Orford to Brookings has been dubbed "the fabulous 50 miles" because of the spectacular rocky coast, with its crashing waves, jutting cliffs, enveloping fogs, and general aura of untouched wilderness. The road winds high above the sea, seeming to teeter dangerously close to the edge and the jagged rocks below. In places, the rainfall reaches 108 inches annually, and there are spots where, it is argued, the sun seldom emerges from its cloudy veil.

South of Port Orford, there is a manmade attraction, the Prehistoric Gardens. Here roam models of dinosaurs in lifelike poses, a slight anachronism since during the era of the thunder lizards the Oregon coast was deep under water.

From here, Highway 101 sticks pretty close to the shoreline as it reaches Gold Beach at the mouth of the Rogue River. This is high-profile tourist country, to a large degree because of the jet boat trips up the Rogue River. The Rogue is world-famous for being wild and scenic, with whitewater rafting thrills the heart-stopper of choice. There's a 64-mile gentle round trip to Ag-ness, an 80-mile round tripper which includes some whitewater rapids, and a real 104-mile high-impact adventure which bounces upriver past a succession of wild rapids until Blossom Bar Rapids becomes too dangerous to allow fur-ther upriver penetration.

Gold Beach is more than jet boats. It's a popular port for ocean fishing and has a generally wild and pristine atmosphere. It became Gold Beach be-cause early arrivers found gold in the sand and streaks of it in the surrounding cliffs. None of it remains today.

Near Brookings, the Samuel H. Boardman State Park, stretching along the coast, becomes the focal point of interest. Some 11 different viewpoints have been scratched out of the rock along the highway, amid towering bluffs, precipitous cliffs, off-shore rock needles and stony arches. There is access to the pocket beaches at low tide with clamming, hiking, and ocean fishing all there for the taking. This primeval spectacle continues until you reach Brook-ings, on the north bank of the Chetco River, and its sister town, Harbor, on the south bank.

Brookings, a picturesque little city, is a constant source of amazement to Oregon natives. It exists in a climate totally isolated from the remainder of the state. When Oregon is freezing, Brookings may be balmy. When the entire state swelters, Brookings is cool. This unusual climate is ideal for the growing of Easter lily bulbs, and it is estimated that Brookings provides 90 percent of all lilies sold in the U.S. Logging, wood products, and commercial fishing are all big here. The Kalmiopsis Wilderness lies to the east in the Siskiyou moun-tains, a target destination for backpackers and hikers.

So the Oregon coast, which began somewhat serenely in the north with the placid sands of Gearhart, becomes progressively wilder, more primitive, less crowded, more challenging as one moves southward. It is not surprising that it retains an inexhaustible and irresistible allure for both visitors and na-tives jaded by the clatter and clutter of civilization.

Photo Credits

Front cover, clockwise: Siletz Pow Wow, Warm Springs Indian Reservation, Shimenak Bridge in Linn County, and wine grower Josef Fleischmann by Joe Bianco.

Page 1, Traditional Indian pole fishing by Joe Bianco.

Page 15, Umatilla Indian Fermore Craig, and moon by Joe Bianco.

Pages 18–19, Siletz Pow Wow by Joe Bianco.

Page 24, Chief Carl Sampson by Joe Bianco.

Page 29, Basque dancers, courtesy Oinkar Basque Dancers, Boise.

Page 39, Timberline Lodge, courtesy Timberline Lodge.

Page 41, Mt. Angel Abbey by Joe Bianco.

Page 44, Mt. Angel Abbey by Joe Bianco.

Page 53, The Harvest Monument (Fruchtsaeule) by Joe Bianco.

Page 57, Covered bridge interior, North Willamette Valley by Joe Bianco.

Page 61, Tara McKnight by Joe Bianco.

Page 64, Winemaking by John Rizzo.

Page 73, Central Oregon near Fossil, courtesy Oregon Tourism Division.

Page 75, John Day Fossil Beds, courtesy Oregon Department of Transportation.

Page 81, Pendleton Round-Up by Howdyshell Photos.

Page 85, Crater Lake, courtesy Oregon Tourism Division.

Page 89, Wolf Creek Inn, courtesy Canyonville Publishers.

Page 91, Tillamook, courtesy Oregon Tourism Division.

Page 95, Bandon lighthouse, courtesy Oregon Tourism Division.

Back cover, Portrait of author by Joe G. Bianco.